Praise for Virgilio Piñera and T

Virgilio Piñera's poetry occupies the fragile spa between disillusion and reality. His poems are quie champions against indifference, affirmations that seek to both grieve over and honor our human existence. Pablo Medina's translations are enduring, necessary treasures.

—**Richard Blanco**, Obama inaugural poet and author of *The Prince of los Cocuyos*

Telluric, absurdist, surrealist, feverishly tropical, Virgilio Piñera's *The Weight of the Island* is a poetic cosmos without parallel. Piñera's voice is disturbing, anguished, dissonant and yet deeply moving. You feel the full emotional and psychological presence of the man in every verse he penned. We can rejoice that the English-speaking public can finally become acquainted with this utterly original poet. Only an artist of Pablo Medina's gifts could have achieved the miracle of bringing Piñera fully alive into English.

—**Jaime Manrique**, author of *Cervantes Street*

Virgilio Piñera has been too long ignored amid a louder, at times discordant music of twentieth century Latin American poetry. This smart selection moves into Piñera's more intimate writing, his personal evocations of love and disillusionment, his closely observed poems of absurd social behaviors and mechanical decorum played out against the certainty of mortality. Yet Piñera's poems are all celebrations of life that break through the stifling silence of our permanent night. Medina's remarkable translations in *The Weight of the Island* now renew his gifts to the world.

—**Douglas Unger**, author of *Voices from Silence*

When we read the poetry of Virgilio Piñera we must try to identify the invisible or the mystery that lies behind his words, for his language is filled with doubt and irony as the Cuban poet works the regions of despair, desolation and loneliness. Medina's translation is vivid and sensitive and becomes a recreation of that poetry rather than a mere translation. If Piñera as a poet translates his desolate life into a poetry which is fierce and bitter, Medina's English rendition captures the vitality of the original Spanish and conveys the fierceness of a poet who felt imprisoned by "the cursed condition of water on all sides."

—**Professor Isabel Alvarez Borland**, author of
Cuban America Literature of Exile: From Person to Persona

Diálogos
Books

The Weight of the Island
La isla en peso

Selected Poems of Virgilio Piñera

Translated by Pablo Medina

The Weight of the Island:
Selected Poems of Virgilio Piñera
Translated by Pablo Medina

Printed in the U.S.A.
First Printing
10 9 8 7 6 5 4 3 2 1   15 16 17 18 19 20

Book design: Bill Lavender.
Back cover photo of Pablo Medina: Jennifer Waddell
Cover artwork and design: Pablo Medina Jr.

Library of Congress Control Number: 2015930121
Piñera, Virgilio
The Weight of the Island: Selected Poems of Virgilio Piñera / Virgilio Piñera;
with Pablo Medina (translator)
p. cm.
Includes Introduction by Pablo Medina
ISBN: 978-1-935084-82-2 (pbk.)

DIÁLOGOS
AN IMPRINT OF LAVENDER INK
DIALOGOSBOOKS.COM

Acknowledgements

I wish to thank Mark Statman and Flora González, who read the manuscript and offered valuable suggestions. Carlos Espinosa Domínguez, Dick Cluster, and Mark Weiss guided me in seeking the rights to the originals. My assistants Eloisa Amezcua and Marisela Navarro worked tirelessly in getting the manuscript ready for publication. For the actual permission to publish these poems in bilingual format, I thank the "herederos of Virgilio Piñera," and for his trust and foresight, I am grateful to Bill Lavender for including *The Weight of the Island* in the Diálogos translation series.

I wish to thank *Ezra: An Online Journal of Translation*, in which some of these translations first appeared.

La isla en peso

de La vida entera

Elegía Así – 22
La isla en peso – 26
Vida de flora – 48
Ah, del hotel – 52
Poema para la poesía – 58
Yo lo veo – 66
Tesis del gabinete azul – 68
Un bamboleo frenético – 70
Sin embargo… – 74
El jardín – 76
Poema para ser dicho en medio de un gran silencio – 82
En el gato tuerto – 84

de Una broma colosal

Lo de menos – 90
Si muero en la carretera – 92
Bueno, digamos – 96
Un duque de Alba – 98
Alocución contra los necrófilos – 100
En resumen – 104
Descansa, descansa – 108
Felizmente un camino – 116
Himno a la vida mía – 118
El hechizado – 122
Me esperan – 124
Y otro día – 126
Naturalmente en 1930 – 128
De nuevo nacer – 130
Dos o tres secretos – 132

The Weight of an Island

Translator's Preface – 10

from All Of Life

Elegy and Such – 23
The Weight of the Island – 27
Life of Flora – 49
Ah, the Hotel – 53
Poem for Poetry – 59
I See It – 67
Thesis of the Blue Cabinet – 69
A Frenetic Sway – 71
Nevertheless – 75
The Garden – 77
Poem to be Said in the Midst of a Great Silence – 83
At the One-Eyed Cat – 85

from A Colossal Joke

The Least of It – 91
If I Die on the Highway – 93
Well, Let Us Say – 97
A Duke of Alba – 99
Against the Necrophiliacs – 101
In Brief – 105
Rest, Rest – 109
Happily a Road – 117
Hymn to My Life – 119
The Magic Man – 123
They Are Waiting – 125
Another Day – 127
Naturally in 1930 – 129
To Be Born Again – 131
Two or Three Secrets – 133

Palabras de joven – 134
Isla – 136

de Poemas desaparecidos

Balada de tu muerte – 140
Los cencerros de la paciencia – 142
Ondean las largas banderas – 144
Nunca los dejaré – 148
En el dentista – 150
Pin, pan, pun – 152
Quien soy – 154
Una niñada de Piñera – 156
¿Se dijo? – 158
De sobremesa – 160
Nadie – 164

To a Young Man – 135
Island – 137

from Disappeared Poems

Ballad of Your Death – 141
The Cow Bells of Patience – 143
Long Flags Waving – 145
I'll Never Leave Them – 149
At the Dentist – 151
Shooting Gallery – 153
Who I Am – 155
Piñera's Inner Child – 157
Was It Said? – 159
Table Talk – 161
No One – 165

Notes on the Poems – 166
Biographies – 167

Translator's Preface

Virgilio Piñera wrote that from an early age he knew three things about himself that would never change: he was poor, he was a homosexual, and he liked art. Born to a middle-class family forever on the verge of financial collapse, Piñera himself never achieved a degree of financial security. Unlike many Cuban writers of his generation who wrote in their off hours, he was incapable of holding a job for very long. Instead he dedicated himself to literature with unbridled passion, producing plays, poems, stories, novels, and criticism. Piñera is now seen, alongside José Lezama Lima, as one of the greatest writers of pre-Revolutionary Cuba. It was not always so.

While his uncompromising devotion to literature won him many followers, his homosexuality won him enemies. He sought neither. He did not hold court in his house as did his archrival Lezama Lima, that other great man of letters in 1950's Havana; nor was he willing to parade his gayness in front of the authorities, like his disciple Reinaldo Arenas. Publically, Piñera was a quiet, reticent man who stayed away from the limelight, much preferring the company of a few friends for whom he'd cook dinner and with whom he'd play long games of canasta.

In his writing he was anything but reticent. Piñera was a versatile man of letters, and he became best known primarily as a playwright who anticipated the theater of the absurd with plays like *Electra Garrigó* and *Falsa alarma (False Alarm)*. His fiction owed much to Kafka, and his poetry suggested Cavafy, but Piñera was a writer with a unique vision molded by his tropical temperament, his peculiar sense of independence, and his marginalization as a gay man in a society—both before and after the Revolution—that considered homosexuality a perversion. His posture was skeptical, his critical eye fierce, his attitude insouciant. He was apolitical but never uncommitted. His early poetic masterpiece, the long poem "La isla en peso" ("The Weight of the Island") is a testament to his historical and social conscience. As Guillermo Cabrera Infante wrote, Piñera's insurrection was always literary.

He was a poet of daily life, of quotidian experience. He once said that literature was nothing more than colossal gossip. Even when writing in form, the language of his poetry was simple and direct, unclouded by literary fashion or pretension. In this he differed markedly from Lezama Lima. The author of *Paradiso*, a monumental novel in which the Cuban baroque reaches its greatest splendor, Lezama was the god of high culture in the literary scene of 1950's Havana. Physically they were opposites. Lezama Lima was a voluminous man, a gourmand of insatiable appetites. Piñera was thin, malnourished because of his chronic poverty, and disinterested in food or drink. Lezama was always dressed in elegant though rumpled linen suits or *guayaberas* while Piñera sported short-sleeved shirts and cheap pants.

They were great smokers—Lezama liked large cigars, Virgilio chained-smoked cigarettes. Both were gay. While Lezama was given to young delicate men, many of them his disciples, Virgilio liked rough, uneducated lovers picked up in seedy bars or in the neighborhood around the port. They were joined by their love of literature and for a brief time, they collaborated in *Orígenes*, the most important Cuban literary magazine of the period. That collaboration was short-lived, however. During a gathering of writers, they had words. Lezama demanded they settle their differences outside. The scene must have been ridiculous—a skinny, reluctant Piñera against the fat, outrageous Lezama. No punches were thrown since Virgilio believed he would win by refusing to fight, but they didn't speak to each other for many years. What remained was a grudging admiration for one another's work, which Piñera described in the poem, "Well, Let Us Say," dedicated to Lezama, as well as the recognition of one another as opposite poles toward which Cuban writing gravitated in a state of constant tension:

We have lived on an island,
perhaps not as we wanted
but as we could.
Even so we tore down some temples
and raised others
that might perhaps last
or themselves be torn down in due time.
We have written without rest,
dreamed enough
to penetrate reality.
We built dykes
against idolatry and decay. . .

Piñera spent much of the late 1940s and 1950s in self-imposed exile in Buenos Aires, Argentina. There he met Borges and his circle. Borges invited him to give a lecture in the Sociedad Argentina de Escritores (Argentine Society of Writers), which the great Argentinian presided over, and Piñera began to publish in Borges's magazine *Sur*. While in Buenos Aires he befriended the Polish writer Wytold Gombrowicz and formed part of the team that translated Gombrowicz's masterpiece *Ferdydurke* into Spanish. Those were heady days in Buenos Aires, a city filled with writers and their literature, where Piñera fit in easily. Nevertheless, he felt lonely and displaced and longed to get back to Havana, which he did just before the triumph of the Revolution in January 1959.

Like many writers, Piñera jumped on the revolutionary bandwagon, accepting a post as a columnist to *Lunes de Revolución*, the cultural section of the official state newspaper, to which he contributed literary criticism and book and theater reviews. He wrote under the pseudonym El Escriba, perhaps pressured by the editors not to reveal his identity and his reputation as a homosexual. It became gradually clear that the Revolution, a male-dominated institution if ever there was one, did not tolerate homosexuality, seeing it as a threat to its attempts to create the New Man. That New Man had to be, according to the tenets of Fidelismo, a model heterosexual. Piñera eventually left *Lunes de Revolución*, and disillusioned by the direction the Revolution had taken, settled in his small house in the beach town of Guanabo to write, visiting his friends in the city occasionally and just as occasionally being visited by them.

In 1961, after the Bay of Pigs disaster, and after Virgilio's return from a European trip, a movie short titled *P.M.*, filmed by Orlando Jiménez Leal and Sabá Cabrera Infante caused a public furor. The movie showed the bar scene of Havana at night—people playing music, dancing, getting drunk. When the movie was shown to the Commission of Film Review to get its approval for release, the Commission confiscated the film. In protest, the directors of *Lunes de Revolución* circulated a manifesto signed by two hundred artists and writers. As a result, Fidel Castro and his cultural apparatchiks organized a series of gatherings to which only writers and artists were invited. Then president Raúl Dorticós asked the audience if there was anything they needed to say, not only about the confiscated film but about the relationship between culture and the Revolution. No one dared stand up, except for a shy, tentative figure, none other than Virgilio Piñera, who walked to the microphone in the aisle and declared, "I want to say that I am very much afraid. I don't know why, but that's all I have to say." Without another word he returned to his seat. In thus manner he expressed what many felt but lacked the courage to say.

A number of unfortunate events unfolded after those gatherings. The film *P.M.* was not only criticized but condemned, *Lunes* was closed, and Cuban culture came under the absolute control of the state. In other words, Cuba, or, better said, the Cuban government, began its Stalinist period, during which many groups were persecuted and suppressed. Later, during a round-up of homosexuals in and around Havana, Piñera was arrested and jailed. His release was negotiated by several of his friends, including the novelist Guillermo Cabrera Infante. Soon after, Piñera abandoned his small beach house in Guanabo and moved to an apartment in the city. He continued writing, but he was not allowed to produce his plays or publish his work. Lezama suffered a similar fate, and it wasn't until well after their deaths that the cultural machinery of the Cuban state saw fit to acknowledge their remarkable contribution to Cuban literature.

Though Piñera's first published work was a collection of poems, *Las furias*, he eventually gave up trying to publish his poetry, but he never stopped writing it. Perhaps his poverty kept him from paying for its publication. More likely, he felt a disenchantment with a certain posture on the part of poets, a condescension coupled with an exquisiteness of language, which set them apart from everyday life. Piñera believed that poetry and everyday existence were inextricably linked. He disdained positioning himself as Poet, and with a logic particularly his own—a poet's logic—he stopped publishing his poems.

Virgilio Piñera was born in the city of Cárdenas, Matanzas, Cuba, in 1912, the second of six children. His family was middle class but forever struggling against poverty. They moved often, following the ineffectual business plans of the father, Juan Manuel Piñera, an engineer by trade. Juan Manuel's failed ambitions made him irascible and unpredictable, forcing Virgilio and his sister Luisa to cower in the presence of their father, avoiding him as much as possible lest they awaken his volcanic temper. They grew up this way, making up quiet theatrical games as they went. As soon as Virgilio was able, he moved away from his family, living in a succession of rooming houses while trying to complete his university studies. The three constants in his life remained, as he had said, his poverty, his gayness, and his love of art. He died of a heart attack in 1979.

As I went about translating Piñera's poetry, New York School poets like Frank O'Hara, Kenneth Koch, and John Ashbery kept coming to mind. I doubt that Piñera ever read them, yet there are undeniable tonal similarities between them, arising out of an attitude I can only describe as emotion reined in by disillusion. The result is the ironic stance cultivated to keep the poet, the urban 20th-century poet, in control of his psyche. Using innocent remarks in a context where such remarks are diminished, if not erased, by harsh reality, the poet begins and ends in disillusion. Here is the opening of Virgilio's "Elegy and Such":

> I invite the word
> walking its barren bark among the dogs.
> Everything is sad.
> If it crowns forehead and breasts with shiny leaves
> a cold smile will blossom on the moon.
> Everything is sad.
> Later the sad dogs will eat the leaves
> and bark out words with glistening sounds.
> Everything is sad.

And here is the opening of Kenneth Koch's poem "Paradiso":

> There is no way not to be excited
> When what you have been disillusioned by raises its head
> From its arms and seems to want to talk to you again.
> You forget home and family
> And set off on foot or in your automobile
> And go to where you believe this form of reality
> May dwell. Not finding it there, you refuse
> Any further contact
> Until you are back again trying to forget
> The only thing that moved you (it seems) and gave what you forever will have
> But in the form of a disillusion.

The struggle between illusion and disillusion is what determines the tonal registers of both poets. Illusion comes easily to lesser poets. Disillusion, the condition that prevails in the modern mind, is another matter. But Koch is of New York, you say, he deserves to be disillusioned. Piñera is of Havana, which, on the surface, is a place of light and warmth, the capital of illusion. Dig a little deeper and you'll find that Havana is the New York of the tropics, where disillusion, as in Cavafy's Alexandria, has always lurked around every corner, inside every bar. Poets will be poets, and if they keep themselves from falling into despair or cynicism (the death of poetry), their poems will explore the territory between illusion, where light might shine, and disillusion, where shadows reign. It is precisely Piñera's exploration of this duality in the objects and events of daily life that first drew me to his long-neglected poetry and led me, after years of reading, to translate his poems.

Translating Piñera presented a number of difficulties, not the least of which is his use of Cubanisms, particularly in the earlier poems. I have included a section titled "Notes on the Poems" at the end of the text that clarifies some of these words and expressions. Also a challenge was his use of the rhythmic patterns of spoken Cuban Spanish, and, more specifically, of the language spoken in Havana during his lifetime. As Auden pointed out, translating the music of poetry is an impossible task, and so, wherever possible, I adopted the rhythms of New York English, hoping to parallel, if not recreate, the intricacies of Piñera's music.

Until now, Piñera's poetry has appeared only sporadically in English translation. The Spanish versions collected in *The Weight of the Island* were taken from *La isla en peso*, the invaluable anthology of Piñera's work edited by Antón Arrufat and published by Tusquets Editores in 2000. With two exceptions, I stayed away from translating Piñera's more formal poems and instead focused on his free verse. I also passed over Piñera's attempts at writing poetry in French, gathered in *La isla en peso* under the section title "Tout un cortège fantasque," since there was nothing in them that Piñera did not attempt in his Spanish poems. In selecting the poems to translate, I was also guided by my own sense of Piñera's world view, which I gathered from my readings of his plays, fiction, critical essays, as well as Carlos Espinosa Domínguez's remarkable biography, *Virgilio Piñera en persona*.

–Pablo Medina, Pine Island, 2014

The Weight of the Island

for Willis Barnstone

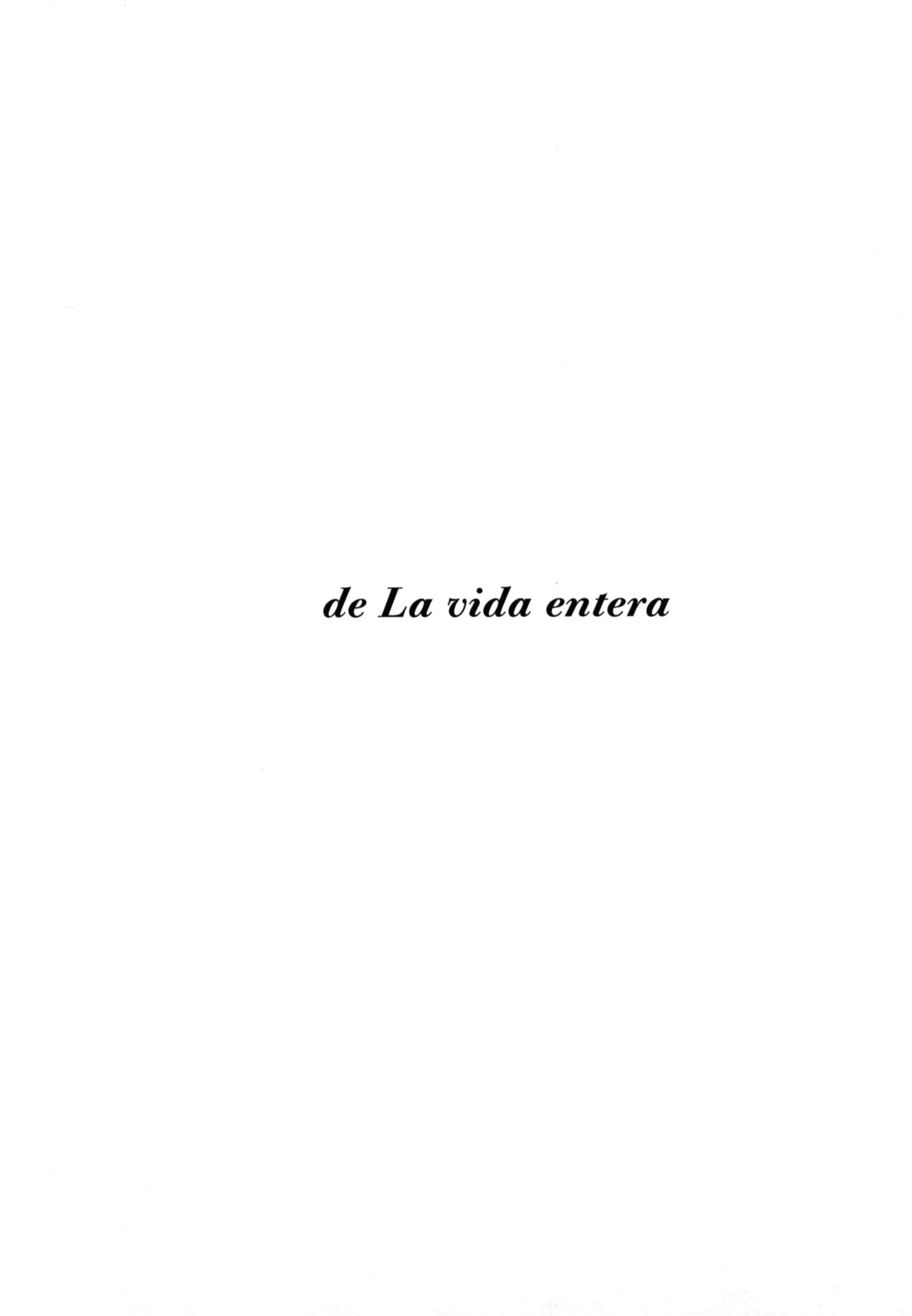

de La vida entera

from All Of Life

Elegía Así

Invito a la palabra
que pasea entre perros su desierto ladrido.
Todo es triste.
Si con lustrosas hojas corona frente y senos
una fría sonrisa florecerá en la luna.
Todo es triste.
Después los perros tristes comerán de las hojas
y ladrarán palabras de lustroso sonido.
Todo es triste.
Un perro invita a los jacintos en el río.
Todo es triste.
Con lunadas palabras, con aperradas flechas,
con dentadas hojuelas
hieren a las mudas doncellas los jacintos.
Todo es triste.
Crece la negra yerba con un rumor tranquilo,
pero lustrosos filos acarician el ritmo.
Todo es triste.
Detrás de las palabras las serpientes se ríen,
la sorda tierra no permite sonidos.
Todo es triste.

Ladra un ave celeste por el cielo
para alejar la muerte.
Con flores de la noche la descubre,
con palabras de perro la seduce,
con una copa de tierra la sepulta.
Todo es triste.
Invito a la terrosa palabra
que perfora la vida y los espejos
y el eco de su imagen dividido.
Todo es triste.
Un juego de palabras con ladridos.

Elegy and Such

I invite the word
walking its barren bark among the dogs.
Everything is sad.
If it crowns forehead and breasts with shining leaves
a cold smile will blossom on the moon.
Everything is sad.
Later the sad dogs will eat the leaves
and bark out words with glistening sounds.
Everything is sad.
A dog invites the hyacinths by the river.
Everything is sad.
With loony words, with doggerel arrows,
with tiny toothy leaves
the hyacinths wound the mute damsels.
Everything is sad.
The black grass grows with a quiet hum,
but shiny edges caress the rhythm.
Everything is sad.
Behind the words the serpents laugh,
deaf earth allows no sound.
Everything is sad.

A heavenly bird barks in the sky
to scare death away.
The bird discovers it with the flowers of night
and seduces it with words of a dog
and buries it with a cupful of earth.
Everything is sad.
I invite the earthbound word
that cuts through life and mirrors
and splits the echo of its image.
Everything is sad.
A play of words and barks.

Todo es triste.
Un venablo con veloz viento vuela
en variaciones viriles
Media copa de tierra enmudeció a la música.

Todo es triste.
Después la tierra se bebió a ella misma.
Todo es triste.
Y cuando llegue el tiempo de la muerte
ponedme ante el espejo para verme.
Todo es triste.

1941

Everything is sad.
A javelin whooshes through the speeding wind
in virile variations.
Half a cup of earth silenced the music.

Everything is sad.
Then the earth drank itself.
Everything is sad.
And when the time for death arrives
place me before a mirror where I may see myself.
Everything is sad.

1941

La isla en peso

La maldita circunstancia del agua por todas partes
me obliga a sentarme en la mesa del café.
Si no pensara que el agua me rodea como un cáncer
hubiera podido dormir a pierna suelta.
Mientras los muchachos se despojaban de sus ropas para nadar
doce personas morían en un cuarto por compresión.
Cuando a la madrugada la pordiosera resbala en el agua
en el preciso momento en que se lava uno de sus pezones,
me acostumbro al hedor del puerto,
me acostumbro a la misma mujer que invariablemente masturba,
noche a noche, al soldado de guardia en medio del sueño de los peces.
Una taza de café no puede alejar mi idea fija,
en otro tiempo yo vivía adánicamente.
¿Qué trajo la metamorfosis?

La eterna miseria que es el acto de recordar.
Si tú pudieras formar de nuevo aquellas combinaciones,
devolviéndome el país sin el agua,
me la bebería toda para escupir al cielo.
Pero he visto la música detenida en las caderas,
he visto a las negras bailando con vasos de ron en sus cabezas.
Hay que saltar del lecho con la firme convicción
de que tus dientes han crecido,
de que tu corazón te saldrá por la boca.
Aún flota en los arrecifes el uniforme del marinero ahogado.
Hay que saltar del lecho y buscar la vena mayor del mar para desangrarlo.
Me he puesto a pescar esponjas frenéticamente,
esos seres milagrosos que pueden desalojar hasta la última gota de agua
y vivir secamente.
Esta noche he llorado al conocer a una anciana
que ha vivido ciento ocho años rodeada de agua por todas partes.
Hay que morder, hay que gritar, hay que arañar.
He dado las últimas instrucciones.

The Weight of the Island

The cursed condition of water on all sides
forces me to sit at a café table.
If I didn't believe that water surrounds me like cancer
I might have slept soundly.
While the boys threw off their clothes to go swimming
twelve people died of suffocation in a single room.
When at dawn the beggar woman slips on the water
just as she is washing one of her nipples,
I grow accustomed to the stench of the port,
I grow accustomed to the same woman who night after night
ceaselessly masturbates the soldier on guard in the midst of the dream of fishes.
A cup of coffee will not erase my fixation,
in other times I lived like Adam.
What brought about the transformation?

The eternal misery of the act of remembering.
If you could shape again those combinations,
giving me back the country without the water,
I would drink it all to spit at the sky.
But I have seen music stopped at the hips,
I have seen black women dance with glasses of rum on their heads.
You must jump out of bed with the firm belief
that your teeth have grown,
that your heart will come out of your mouth.
The uniform of a drowned sailor still floats on the reef.
You must jump out of bed and seek the major vein to bleed out the sea.
Frantically I fish for sponges,
those miraculous creatures that can soak up the last drop ofwater
and live dryly.
Tonight I have wept after meeting an old lady
who has lived for a hundred and eight years surrounded by water on all sides.
You must bite, you must scream, you must scratch.
I've given the final instructions.

El perfume de la piña puede detener a un pájaro.
Los once mulatos se disputaban el fruto,
los once mulatos fálicos murieron en la orilla de la playa.
He dado las últimas instrucciones.
Todos nos hemos desnudado.

Llegué cuando daban un vaso de aguardiente a la virgen bárbara,
cuando regaban ron por el suelo y los pies parecían lanzas,
justamente cuando un cuerpo en el lecho podría parecer impúdico,
justamente en el momento en que nadie cree en Dios.
Los primeros acordes y la antigüedad de este mundo:
hieráticamente una negra y una blanca y el líquido al saltar.
Para ponerme triste me huelo debajo de los brazos.
Es en este país donde no hay animales salvajes.
Pienso en los caballos de los conquistadores cubriendo a las yeguas,
pienso en el desconocido son del areíto
desaparecido para toda la eternidad,
ciertamente debo esforzarme a fin de poner en claro
el primer contacto carnal en este país, y el primer muerto.
Todos se ponen serios cuando el timbal abre la danza.
Solamente el europeo leía las meditaciones cartesianas.
El baile y la isla rodeada de agua por todas partes:
plumas de flamencos, espinas de pargo, ramos de albahaca, semillas de aguacate.
La nueva solemnidad de esta isla.
¡País mío, tan joven, no sabes definir!

¿Quién puede reír sobre esta roca fúnebre de los sacrificios de gallos?
Los dulces ñáñigos bajan sus puñales acompasadamente.
Como una guanábana un corazón puede ser traspasado sin cometer crimen.
Una mano en el *tres* puede traer todo el siniestro color de los caimitos
más lustrosos que un espejo en el relente,
sin embargo el bello aire se aleja de los palmares.
Si hundieras los dedos en su pulpa creerías en la música.
Mi madre fue picada por un alacrán cuando estaba embarazada.

¿Quién puede reír sobre esta roca de los sacrificios de gallo?

The odor of pineapple can stop a bird.
Eleven mulattoes fought over the fruit,
eleven phallic mulattoes died on the shore.
I've given the last instructions.
We've all taken off our clothes.

I arrived when they were giving the barbarian virgin a glass of firewater,
when they sprayed rum on the ground and feet seemed like lances,
just as a body in bed could seem shameless,
just at the moment when no one believes in God.
The first chords and the antiquity of this world:
hieratically a black woman and a white woman and the liquid jumping.
To get depressed I smell my armpits
This is a country without wild animals.
I think of the conquistadors' stallions mounting their mares,
I think of the unknown music of the *areíto* lost for eternity,
I should certainly make an effort to shed light on the first
carnal contact in this country, and the first death.
Everyone gets serious when the kettle drum opens the dance.
Only the Europeans read Cartesian meditations.
The dance and the island surrounded by water on all sides:
flamingo feathers, red snapper bones, branches of basil, seeds of avocado.
The new solemnity of this island.
Country of mine, so young, you know nothing of definitions!

Who can laugh over this funereal rock on which roosters are sacrificed?
The sweet *ñáñigos* lower their daggers in rhythm.
Like a soursop a heart can be run through without committing a crime.
A hand on the *tres* can bring all the sinister color of star apples
shinier than a mirror in mist;
nevertheless, the beautiful song retreats from the palm trees.
If you sank your fingers in its pulp you'd believe in music.
My mother was stung by a scorpion when she was pregnant.

Who can laugh over this rock on which roosters are sacrificed?
Who can contain himself when the *claves* clack?

¿Quién se tiene a sí mismo cuando las claves chocan?
¿Quién desdeña ahogarse en la indefinible llamarada del flamboyán?
La sangre adolescente bebemos en las pulidas jícaras.
Ahora no pasa un tigre sino su descripción.

Las blancas dentaduras perforando la noche,
y también los famélicos dientes de los chinos esperando el desayuno
después de la doctrina cristiana.
Todavía puede esta gente salvarse del cielo,
pues al compás de los himnos las doncellas agitan diestramente
los falos de los hombres.
La impetuosa ola invade el extenso salón de las genuflexiones.
Nadie piensa en implorar, en dar gracias, en agradecer, en testimoniar.
La santidad se desinfla en una carcajada.
Sean los caóticos símbolos del amor los primeros objetos que palpe,
afortunadamente desconocemos la voluptuosidad y la caricia francesa,
desconocemos el perfecto gozador y la mujer pulpo,
desconocemos los espejos estratégicos,
no sabemos llevar la sífilis con la reposada elegancia de un cisne,
desconocemos que muy pronto vamos a practicar estas mortales elegancias.
Los cuerpos en la misteriosa llovizna tropical,
en la llovizna diurna, en la llovizna nocturna, siempre en lallovizna,
los cuerpos abriendo sus millones de ojos,
los cuerpos, dominados por la luz, se repliegan
ante el asesinato de la piel,
los cuerpos, devorando oleadas de luz, revientan como girasoles de fuego
encima de las aguas estáticas,
los cuerpos, en las aguas, como carbones apagados derivan hacia el mar.

Es la confusión, es el terror, es la abundancia,
es la virginidad que comienza a perderse.
Los mangos podridos en el lecho del río ofuscan mi razón,
y escalo el árbol más alto para caer como un fruto.
Nada podría detener este cuerpo destinado a los cascos de los caballos,
turbadoramente cogido entre la poesía y el sol.

Who can disdain throwing himself in the indescribable flames of the poinciana?
We drink adolescent blood from polished gourds.
Not a tiger passes by now but its description.

The white dentures perforating night,
as well as the famished teeth of Chinamen awaiting breakfast
after Christian doctrine.
These people can still save themselves from heaven
since the damsels stroke expertly
the phalluses of men
to the rhythm of hymns.
The restless wave invades the large hall of the genuflections.
No one thinks of implorations, of gratitude, of gratefulness, of testimonials.
Holiness deflates into laughter.
Even if the chaotic symbols of love are the first objects I touch,
fortunately we do not know the voluptuous French caress,
we do not know the perfect pleasure seeker or the octopus woman,
we do not know the strategic mirror,
we do not know how to bear syphilis with the calm elegance of a swan,
we do not know that very soon we will practice this mortal elegance.
Bodies in the mysterious tropical drizzle,
in the day drizzle and the night drizzle, always in the drizzle,
bodies opening their million eyes,
bodies dominated by light retreat
before the murder of skin,
bodies devouring waves of light burst like sunflowers of fire
over the static waters,
bodies in water, like smothered coals floating out to sea.

It is confusion, it is terror, it is abundance,
it is virginity beginning to be lost.
The rotten mangos on the riverbed confuse my reason,
and I climb the tallest tree to fall like a piece of fruit.
Nothing could stop this body destined for the hooves of horses,
trapped in the confusion between poetry and the sun.

Escolto bravamente el corazón traspasado,
clavo el estilete más agudo en la nuca de los durmientes.
El trópico salta y su chorro invade mi cabeza
pegada duramente contra la costra de la noche.
La piedad original de las auríferas arenas
ahoga sonoramente las yeguas españolas,
la tromba desordena las crines más oblicuas.

No puedo mirar con estos ojos dilatados.
Nadie sabe mirar, contemplar, desnudar un cuerpo.
Es la espantosa confusión de una mano en lo verde,
los estranguladores viajando en la franja del iris.
No sabría poblar de miradas el solitario curso del amor.

Me detengo en ciertas palabras tradicionales:
el aguacero, la siesta, el cañaveral, el tabaco,
con simple ademán, apenas si onomatopéyicamente,
titánicamente paso por encima de su música,
y digo: el agua, el mediodía, el azúcar, el humo.

Yo combino:
el aguacero pega en el lomo de los caballos,
la siesta atada a la cola de un caballo,
el cañaveral devorando a los caballos,
los caballos perdiéndose sigilosamente
en la tenebrosa emanación del tabaco,
el último gesto de los siboneyes mientras el humo pasa por la horquilla
como la carreta de la muerte,
el último ademán de los siboneyes,
y cavo esta tierra para encontrar los ídolos y hacerme una historia.

Los pueblos y sus historias en boca de todo el pueblo.

De pronto, el galeón cargado de oro se mete en la boca
de uno de los narradores,
y Cadmo, desdentado, se pone a tocar el bongó.

I am the brave guard of the pierced heart,
I thrust the sharpest stiletto in the nape of those who sleep.
The tropics jump out and the jet invades my head
stuck dryly to the scab of night.
The initial mercy of golden sands
drowns loudly the Spanish mares,
a waterspout shakes the most oblique manes.

I cannot see with these dilated eyes.
No one knows how to see, consider, unclothe a body.
It is the confusing terror of a hand inside green matter,
stranglers traveling on the arc of the iris.
I couldn't populate with looks the solitary course of love.

I stop at certain traditional words:
squall, siesta, cane field, tobacco,
with a simple gesture, barely onomatopoeic,
I pass with great effort over their music
and I say: water, midday, sugar, smoke.

I combine:
the squall hitting the backs of horses,
the siesta tied to the tail of a horse,
the cane field devouring the horses,
the horses getting silently lost
in the shadowy emanation of tobacco,
the last gesture of the Siboneyes while smoke passes through the yoke
like the cart of death,
the last gesture of the Siboneyes,
and I dig this earth to find idols and make myself a history.

The towns and their history in the mouth of a whole people.

Suddenly a gold-laden galleon enters the mouth
of one of the narrators
and a toothless Cadmus begins to play bongos.

La vieja tristeza de Cadmo y su perdido prestigio:
en una isla tropical los últimos glóbulos rojos de un dragón
tiñen con imperial dignidad el manto de una decadencia.

Las historias eternas frente a la historia de una vez del sol,
las eternas historias de estas tierras paridoras de bufones y cotorras,
las eternas historias de los negros que fueron,
y de los blancos que no fueron,
o al revés o como os parezca mejor,
las eternas historias blancas, negras, amarillas, rojas, azules,
–toda la gama cromática reventando encima de mi cabeza en llamas–,
la eterna historia de la cínica sonrisa del europeo
llegado para apretar las tetas de mi madre.
En horroroso paseo circular,
el tenebroso juego de los pies sobre la arena circular,
el envenado movimiento del talón que rehúye el abanico del erizo,
los siniestros manglares, como un cinturón canceroso,
dan la vuelta a la isla,
los manglares y la fétida arena
aprietan los riñones de los moradores de la isla.

Solo se eleva un flamenco absolutamente.

¡Nadie puede salir, nadie puede salir!
La vida del embudo y encima la nata de la rabia.
Nadie puede salir:
el tiburón más diminuto rehusaría transportar un cuerpo intacto.
Nadie puede salir:
una uva caleta en la frente de la criolla
que se abanica lánguida en una mecedora,
y «nadie puede salir» termina espantosamente en el choque de las claves.
Cada hombre comiendo fragmentos de la isla,
cada hombre devorando los frutos, las piedras y el excremento nutridor,
cada hombre mordiendo el sitio dejado por su sombra,
cada hombre lanzando dentelladas en el vacío donde el sol se acostumbra,
cada hombre, abriendo su boca como una cisterna, embalsa el agua

The old sadness of Cadmus and his lost prestige:
on a tropical island the last red corpuscles of a dragon
stain the cloak of decadence with imperial dignity.

The eternal histories before the one-time history of the sun,
the eternal histories of these lands that breed buffoons and parrots,
the eternal histories of the blacks who were,
of the whites who were not,
or vice versa, or whatever seems best,
the eternal histories, white, black, yellow, red, blue–
the whole gamut of colors exploding over my head in flames–
the eternal history of the cynical smile of the European
who's come to squeeze my mother's tits.
The horrible circular path,
the shadowy play of the feet on the circular sand,
the poisoned movement of the heel that flees from the fan of the sea urchin,
the sinister mangroves surrounding the island
like a cancerous belt,
the mangroves and the fetid sand
squeezing the kidneys of the island's people.

Only a flamingo rises into the absolute.

No one can leave, no one can leave!
The life of a funnel and over it the cream of wrath.
No one can leave:
the smallest shark refuses to carry off a whole body.
No one can leave:
sea grape on the forehead of the creole woman
fanning herself lazily on a rocking chair,
and "no one can leave" ends in the terror of the clack of *claves.*
Every man eating chunks of island,
every man devouring fruit, stones, nutritious excrement,
every man biting the space left by his shadow,
every man hurling teeth into the void where the sun lies down,
every man opening his mouth like a cistern gathers sea water

del mar, pero como el caballo del barón de Munchausen,
la arroja patéticamente por su cuarto trasero,
cada hombre en el rencoroso trabajo de recortar
los bordes de la isla más bella del mundo,
cada hombre tratando de echar a andar a la bestia cruzada de cocuyos.

La bestia es perezosa como un bello macho
y terca como una hembra primitiva.
Verdad es que la bestia atraviesa diariamente los cuatro momentos caóticos,
los cuatro momentos en que se la puede contemplar
–con la cabeza metida entre sus patas– escrutando el horizonte con ojo atroz,
los cuatro momentos en que se abre el cáncer:
madrugada, mediodía, crepúsculo y noche.

Las primeras gotas de una lluvia áspera golpean su espalda
hasta que la piel toma la resonancia de dos maracas pulsadas diestramente.
En este momento, como una sábana o como un pabellón de tregua, podría
desplegarse un agradable misterio,
pero la avalancha de verdes lujuriosos ahoga los mojados sones,
y la monotonía invade el envolvente túnel de las hojas.

El rastro luminoso de un sueño mal parido,
un carnaval que empieza con el canto del gallo,
la neblina cubriendo con su helado disfraz el escándalo de la sabana,
cada palma derramándose insolente en un verde juego de aguas,
perforan, con un triángulo incandescente, el pecho de los primeros aguadores,
y la columna de agua lanza sus vapores a la cara del sol cosida por un gallo.
Es la hora terrible.
Los devoradores de neblina se evaporan
hacia la parte más baja de la ciénaga,
y un caimán los pasa dulcemente a ojo.
Es la hora terrible.
La última salida de la luz de Yara
empuja los caballos contra el fango.
Es la hora terrible.

but, like Baron Munchausen's horse,
he hurls it pathetically out his behind,
every man in his rancor working to cut away
the borders of the most beautiful island on earth,
every man trying to get moving the beast mottled by fireflies.

The beast is lazy like a beautiful male
and stubborn like a primitive female.
It is true that the beast crosses daily the four moments of chaos,
the four moments when it can be observed
—head between its legs—scrutinizing the horizon with a terrible eye,
the four moments when cancer unfolds:
dawn, midday, dusk, and night.

The first drops of a rough rain beat on its back
until the skin takes on the resonance of two maracas expertly shaken.
At that moment, like a bed sheet or a truce pavilion,
a pleasant mystery might spread,
but the avalanche of lecherous greens drowns the wet songs,
and monotony invades the enveloping tunnel of leaves.

The luminous trail of an ill-born dream,
a carnival that begins with the rooster's crow,
the fog covering the scandal of the savanna with its icy disguise,
each palm tree spilling insolence on the green play of waters
all perforate, with a burning triangle, the chest of the first water bearers,
while a column of water hurls its vapors at the sun's face sewn by a rooster.
It is the terrible hour.
The eaters of fog evaporate
toward the lowest part of the swamp,
and an alligator stares at them sweetly with his eyes.
It is the terrible hour.
The light of Yara leaving for the last time
drives the horses against the mud.
It is the terrible hour.

Como un bólido la espantosa gallina cae,
y todo el mundo toma su café.
¿Qué puede el sol en un pueblo tan triste?
Las faenas del día se enroscan al cuello de los hombres
mientras la leche cae desesperadamente.
¿Qué puede el sol en un pueblo tan triste?
Con un lujo mortal los macheteros abren grandes claros en el monte,
la tristísima iguana salta barrocamente en un caño de sangre,
los macheteros, introduciendo cargas de claridad, se van ensombreciendo
hasta adquirir el tinte de un subterráneo egipcio.
¿Quién puede esperar clemencia en esta hora?
Confusamente un pueblo escapa de su propia piel
adormeciéndose con la claridad,
la fulminante droga que puede iniciar un sueño mortal
en los bellos ojos de hombres y mujeres,
en los inmensos y tenebrosos ojos de estas gentes
por los cuales la piel entra a no sé qué extraños ritos.

La piel, en esta hora, se extiende como un arrecife
y muerde su propia limitación,
la piel se pone a gritar como una loca, como una puerca cebada,
la piel trata de tapar su claridad con pencas de palma,
con yaguas traídas distraídamente por el viento,
la piel se tapa furiosamente con cotorras y pitahayas,
absurdamente se tapa con sombrías hojas de tabaco
y con restos de leyendas tenebrosas,
y cuando la piel no es sino una bola oscura,
la espantosa gallina pone un huevo blanquísimo.

¡Hay que tapar! ¡Hay que tapar!
Pero la claridad avanzada, invade
perversamente, oblicuamente, perpendicularmente,
la claridad es una enorme ventosa que chupa la sombra,
y las manos van lentamente hacia los ojos.
Los secretos más inconfesables son dichos:
la claridad mueve las lenguas,

The hideous hen drops like a meteor,
and everyone is having coffee.
What can the sun do with such sad people?
Daily chores curl around the neck of men
while milk falls desperately.
What can the sun do among such sad people?
With deadly luxury the machete men open large clearings in the forest,
a very sad iguana jumps baroquely into a channel of blood,
the machete men introduce loads of clarity and themselves grow dark
until they acquire the hue of an underworld Egyptian.
Who can hope for clemency at this hour?
A confused people flee from their own skin
falling asleep from the clarity,
the explosive drug that can inspire a deadly dream
in the beautiful eyes of men and women,
in the huge, shadowy eyes of these people
through which skin enters who-knows-what strange rites.

At this hour the skin spreads like a reef
and bites its own limitation,
the skin begins screaming like a madwoman, like a greased sow,
the skin tries to cover its clarity with palm fronds,
with pieces of bark brought carelessly by the wind,
the skin covers itself furiously with parrots and dragon fruit,
absurdly it covers itself with shadowy tobacco leaves
and the remains of shadow legends,
and when the skin is nothing but a dark ball,
the hideous hen lays the whitest egg.

Things must be covered! Things must be covered!
But clarity advances, invades
perversely, obliquely, vertically,
clarity is a huge organ that sucks up the shadows
and the hands go slowly toward the eyes.
The most unconfessable secrets are revealed:
clarity moves tongues,

la claridad mueve los brazos,
la claridad se precipita sobre un frutero de guayabas,
la claridad se precipita sobre los negros y los blancos,
la claridad golpea a sí misma,
va de uno a otro lado convulsivamente,
empieza a estallar, a reventar, a rajarse,
la claridad empieza el alumbramiento más horroroso,
la claridad empieza a parir claridad.
Son las doce del día.

Todo un pueblo puede morir de luz como morir de peste.
Al mediodía el monte se puebla de hamacas invisibles,
y, echados, los hombres semejan hojas a la deriva sobre aguas metálicas.
En esta hora nadie sabría pronunciar el nombre más querido,
ni levantar una mano para acariciar un seno;
en esta hora del cáncer un extranjero llegado de playas remotas
preguntaría inútilmente qué proyectos tenemos
o cuántos hombres mueren de enfermedades tropicales en esta isla.
Nadie lo escucharía: las palmas de las manos vueltas hacia arriba,
los oídos obturados por el tapón de la somnolencia,
los poros tapiados con la cera de un fastidio elegante
y de la mortal deglución de las glorias pasadas.

¿Dónde encontrar en este cielo sin nubes el trueno
cuyo estampido raje, de arriba abajo, el tímpano de los durmientes?
¿Qué concha paleolítica reventaría con su bronco cuerno el tímpano de los durmientes?
Los hombres-conchas, los hombres-macaos, los hombres-túneles.
¡Pueblo mío, tan joven, no sabes ordenar!
¡Pueblo mío, divinamente retórico, no sabes relatar!

Como la luz o la infancia aún no tienes un rostro.
De pronto el mediodía se pone en marcha,
se pone en marcha dentro de sí mismo,
el mediodía estático se mueve, se balancea,
el mediodía empieza a elevarse flatulentamente,

clarity moves arms,
clarity falls on a fruit bowl filled with guavas,
clarity falls on black and white alike,
clarity slaps itself around,
moves convulsively from side to side,
begins to explode, burst, crack,
clarity begins the most horrible enlightenment,
clarity gives birth to more clarity.
It's twelve noon.

A whole people can die of light as they can die of the plague.
At noon the forest fills with invisible hammocks
and on them humans are like leaves floating on metallic waters.
At this hour no one might know how to say the most beloved name
or raise a hand to touch a breast;
at this hour of cancer a stranger who comes from distant lands
might ask uselessly what projects we have
or how many people die of tropical diseases on this island.
No one would listen; the hands turned up,
the ears stopped up by the plug of somnolence,
the pores sealed with the wax of an elegant annoyance
and the deadly meal of past glories.

Where to find thunder in this sky without clouds
whose peal splits the eardrum of sleepers from top to bottom?
What Paleolithic conch would burst the eardrum of sleepers with its craggy sound?
The conch-men, the Macao-men, the tunnel-men.
My people, so young, you don't know how to organize!
My people, divinely rhetorical, you don't know how to tell stories!

Like light or infancy you still don't have a face.
Suddenly noon gets going,
gets going inside itself,
static noon moves, balances,
a flatulent noon begins to rise,
its seams are in danger of bursting,

sus costuras amenazan reventar,
el mediodía sin cultura, sin gravedad, sin tragedia,
el mediodía orinando hacia arriba,
orinando en sentido inverso a la gran orinada
de Gargantúa en las torres de Notre Dame,
y todas esas historias, leídas por un isleño que no sabe
lo que es un cosmos resuelto.

Pero el mediodía se resuelve en crepúsculo y el mundo se perfila.
A la luz del crepúsculo una hoja de yagruma ordena su terciopelo,
su color plateado del envés es el primer espejo.
La bestia lo mira con su ojo atroz.
En este trance la pupila se dilata, se extiende
hasta aprehender la hoja.
Entonces la bestia recorre con su ojo las formas sembradas en su lomo
y los hombres tirados contra su pecho.
Es la hora única para mirar la realidad en esta tierra.

No una mujer y un hombre frente a frente,
sino el contorno de una mujer y un hombre frente a frente,
entran ingrávidos en el amor,
de tal modo que Newton huye avergonzado.

Una guinea chilla para indicar el ángelus:
abrus precatorious, anona myristica, anona palustris.

Una letanía vegetal sin trasmundo se eleva
frente a los arcos floridos del amor:
Eugenia aromática, eugenia fragrans, eugenia plicatula.
El paraíso y el infierno estallan y sólo queda la tierra:
Ficus religiosa, ficus nitida, ficus suffocans.
La tierra produciendo por los siglos de los siglos:
Panicum colonum, panicum sanguinale, panicum maximum.

El recuerdo de una poesía natural, no codificada, me viene a los labios:

noon without culture, without gravity, without tragedy,
noon pissing upwards,
pissing opposite the great urination
of Gargantua from the towers of Notre Dame,
and all those stories read by an islander who doesn't know
what a defined cosmos is.

But noon defines itself at dusk and the world gains a profile.
By the light of dusk a yagruma leaf arranges its velvet,
the silver color of the underleaf is the first mirror.
The beast looks at it with an atrocious eye.
In its trance the pupil dilates, opens
until it fixes on the leaf.
Then the beast runs its eye over the forms planted on its back
and the men thrown against its chest.
It's the only time to look at reality in this land.

Not a woman and a man face to face,
but the contour of a man and woman face to face,
they enter weightless into love,
so that Newton runs away in shame.

A guinea hen squeals to announce the Angelus:
abrus precatorius, anona myristica, anona palustris.

A vegetable litany rises without another world
before the flowery arches of love:
Eugenia aromatica, eugenia fragrans, eugenia plicatula.
Paradise and hell explode and only the earth remains:
Ficus religiosa, ficus nitida, ficus sufocans.
Earth producing century after century:
Panicum colonum, panicum sanguinale, panicum maximum.

The recollection of a natural poetry, uncodified, comes to my lips:
Tree of the poet, tree of love, tree of the brain.

Árbol de poeta, árbol del amor, árbol del seso.

Una poesía exclusivamente de la boca como la saliva:
Flor de calentura, flor de cera, flor de la Y.

Una poesía microscópica:
Lágrimas de Job, lágrimas de Júpiter, lágrimas de amor.

Pero la noche se cierra sobre la poesía y las formas se esfuman.
En esta isla lo primero que la noche hace es despertar el olfato:
todas las aletas de todas las narices azotan el aire
buscando una flor invisible;
la noche se pone a moler millares de pétalos,
la noche se cruza de paralelos y meridianos de olor,
los cuerpos se encuentran en el olor,
se reconocen en este olor único que nuestra noche sabe provocar;
el olor lleva la batuta de las cosas que pasan por la noche,
el olor entra en el baile, se aprieta contra el güiro,
el olor sale por la boca de los instrumentos musicales,
se posa en el pie de los bailadores,
el corro de los presentes devora cantidades de olor,
abre la puerta y las parejas se suman a la noche.
La noche es un mango, es una piña, es un jazmín,
la noche es un árbol frente a otro árbol sin mover sus ramas,
la noche es un insulto perfumado en la mejilla de la bestia;
una noche esterilizada, una noche sin almas en pena,
sin memoria, sin historia, una noche antillana;
una noche interrumpida por el europeo,
el inevitable personaje de paso que deja su cagada ilustre,
a lo sumo, quinientos años, un suspiro en el rodar de la noche antillana,
una excrecencia vencida por el olor de la noche antillana.
No importa que sea una procesión, una conga,
una comparsa, un desfile.
La noche invade con su olor y todos quieren copular.
El olor sabe arrancar las máscaras de la civilización,
sabe que el hombre y la mujer se encontrarán sin falta en el platanal.

A poetry exclusively of the mouth, like saliva:
fever flower, wax flower, Y-flower.

A microscopic poetry:
tears of Job, tears of Jupiter, tears of love.

But night closes on poetry and shapes disappear.
On this island the first thing night does is awaken the sense of smell:
all the flared noses suck up the air
searching for an invisible flower;
night grinds up thousands of petals,
night is crisscrossed by the parallels and meridians of smell,
bodies find one another through smell,
they recognize each other in the unique smell our night knows to provoke;
smell holds the baton of things that happen at night,
smell enters the dance, tightens against the *güiro*,
smell goes out the mouths of musical instruments,
lands on the feet of the dancers,
those present devour quantities of smell.
Smell opens the door and the couples spill into the night.
Night is a mango, a pineapple, a jasmine flower,
night is a tree in front of another tree with motionless branches.
night is a perfumed insult on the cheek of the beast;
a sterilized night, a night without sorrowful souls,
without memory or history, an Antilles night;
a night interrupted by the European,
the inevitable character passing by who leaves his illustrious turd,
at most, five hundred years, a mere sigh in the rolling Antilles night,
an excretion defeated by the smell of the Antilles night.
It doesn't matter that it's a procession, a conga,
a carnival, a parade.
Night invades with its smell and everyone wants to have sex.
The smell knows how to tear away the masks of civilization,
knows that man and woman will find one another in the banana grove.
Muse of paradise, protect the lovers!

¡Musa paradisíaca, ampara a los amantes!

No hay que ganar el cielo para gozarlo,
dos cuerpos en el platanal valen tanto como la primera pareja,
la odiosa pareja que sirvió para marcar la separación.
¡Musa paradisíaca, ampara a los amantes!

No queremos potencias celestiales sino presencias terrestres,
que la tierra nos ampare, que nos ampare el deseo,
felizmente no llevamos el cielo en la masa de la sangre,
sólo sentimos su realidad física
por la comunicación de la lluvia al golpear nuestras cabezas.

Bajo la lluvia, bajo el olor, bajo todo lo que es una realidad,
un pueblo se hace y se deshace dejando los testimonios:
un velorio, un guateque, una mano, un crimen,
revueltos, confundidos, fundidos en la resaca perpetua,
haciendo leves saludos, enseñando los dientes, golpeando sus riñones,
un pueblo desciende resuelto en enormes postas de abono
sintiendo cómo el agua lo rodea por todas partes,
más abajo, más abajo, y el mar picando en sus espaldas;
un pueblo permanece junto a su bestia en la hora de partir,
aullando en el mar, devorando frutas, sacrificando animales,
siempre más abajo, hasta saber el peso de su isla;
el peso de una isla en el amor de un pueblo.

1943

One need not earn heaven to enjoy it,
two bodies in the banana grove are as valid as the first couple,
the hateful couple who served to mark the separation,
Muse of paradise, protect the lovers!

We do not want celestial powers but an earthly presence,
let the earth protect us and desire protect us,
happily we do not carry heaven in the mass of our blood,
we only feel its physical reality,
the way that rain communicates with us by beating on our heads.

Under the rain, under the smell, under everything that is reality,
a people make and unmake themselves leaving behind their testimony:
a wake, a party, a hand, a crime,
mixed together, confused, forged in eternal tides,
saying brief hellos, showing their teeth, beating their kidneys,
a people descend defined by huge layers of fertilizer,
sensing how water surrounds them on all sides,
lower, lower and the sea beating their backs;
a people remain next to their beast at the time of departure,
howling in the sea, devouring fruit, sacrificing animals,
always lower, until they know the weight of their island;
the weight of an island in the love of a people.

1943

Vida de flora

Tú tenías grandes pies y un tacón jorobado.
Ponte la flor. Espérame que vamos juntos de viaje.

Tú tenías grandes pies. ¡Qué tristeza en el aire!
¿Quién se mordía la cola? ¿Quién cantaba ese aire?

Tú tenías grandes pies, mi amiga en seco parada.
Una gran luz te brotaba. De los pies, digo, te brotaba,
y sin que nadie lo supiera te fue sorbiendo la nada.

Un gran ruido se sentía en tu cuarto. ¿A Flora qué le pasa?
Nada, que sus grandes pies ocupan todo el espacio.
Sí, tú tenías, tenías la imponderable amargura de un zapato.

Ibas y venías entre dos calientes planchas:
Flora, mucho cuidado, que tus pies son muy grandes,
y la peletería te contrata para exhibir sus hormas gigantes.

Flora, cuántas veces recorrías el barrio
pidiendo un poco de aceite y el brillo de la luna te encantaba.
De pronto subían tus dos monstruos a la cama,
tus monstruos horrorizados por una cucaracha.

Flora, tus medias rojas cuelgan como lenguas de ahorcados.
¿En qué pies poner estas huérfanas? ¿Adónde tus últimos zapatos?

Oye, Flora: tus pies no caben en el río que te ha de conducir a la nada,
al país en que no hay grandes pies ni pequeñas manos ni ahorcados.
Tu querías que te tocaran el tambor para que las aves bajaran,
las aves cantando entre tus dedos mientras el tambor repicaba.
Un aire feroz ondulando por la rigidez de tus plantas,
todo eso que tú pensabas cuando la plancha te doblegaba.

Life of Flora

You had large feet and a twisted heel.
Wear a flower. Wait, let's go on a trip together.

You had large feet. Such sadness in the air!
Who bit her own tail? Who sang that air?

You had large feet, my dear friend stopped dead.
A great light came from you. From your feet, I mean, it spread,
and before we knew it, the void inhaled you like bread.

We heard a loud noise come from your room. What's wrong with Flora?
Nothing, her feet are taking up space.
You, yes, you suffered the unthinkable bitterness of a single shoe.

You came and went between two hot flat irons:
Flora, be careful, your feet are very large,
the shoe store might hire you to model their giant wares.

Flora, many times you walked around the block
to borrow a little oil, in love with the light of the moon.
Suddenly your two monsters climbed on the bed,
your monsters terrified by a roach.

Flora, your red stockings hang like the tongues of two hanged men.
What other feet will slip into those orphaned stockings? Who will take your last shoes?

Listen, Flora: your feet will not fit in the river that leads to the void,
the country where there are no large feet or small hands or hanged men.
You wanted a drum to beat in order to have the birds descend,
the birds singing on your fingers while the drum played.
A fierce wind blew over your stiff soles.
It was all you thought about when the iron flattened you.

Flora, te voy a acompañar hasta tu última morada.
Tú tenías grandes pies y un tacón jorobado.

1944

Flora, I'll go with you to your final resting place,
you with your large feet and a twisted heel.

1944

Ah, del hotel

I.

¿Es una cadena?
Por la tarde empieza el tribunal
y las acometidas del león son cada vez más furiosas.
¿Es realmente una cadena?
El túnel pasa y vuelve a pasar ante el tribunal
con sus pitazos envueltos en un tapiz amarillo.
¿Una cadena con sus eslabones?
Hoy van a juzgar al león.
Tú, el girón del brazo derecho, ve y prosternate
hasta que el manicomio en pleno haya entrado en el túnel.

¿Pasaba una muchacha de falsa doncellez?
¿Pasaban las espantosas viejas del salón verde?
Y tú, tribunal, agita la campanilla, tribunal mío, agítala con furia
que acaba de bajar el ascensor.
¿Quiere subir conmigo?
Es que realmente tengo tanto valor
que desearía acompañar a los que saldrán esta noche.
Pero no acaban de decirnos dónde seremos juzgados,
sí, el león sabe dónde serán oídos sus descargos,
pero es él ciertamente el rey de los animales,
y yo digo, nosotros, los moradores de este hotel
con su túnel circulando sin la menor piedad.
Es notable, las voces no logran subir más arriba del primer piso,
y yo sé que hay gente aguardando ciertas llamadas…
Dicen que el león saldrá absuelto.
Entretanto demos una vuelta por la barriada.

¿Te fijas acaso en los árboles o más bien en la lengua del túnel
que sale por esa ventana?
No sé si realmente es una cadena.
De pronto anuncian con voz estentórea:

Ah, the Hotel

I.

Is it a chain?
The trial begins in the afternoon.
The lion's attacks grow increasingly fierce.
Is it really a chain?
The tunnel passes and passes again before the magistrates
with their whistles wrapped in a yellow tapestry.
A chain with links?
Today they are going to judge the lion.
You, with the tear on the right arm, kneel down
until the whole insane asylum enters the tunnel.

Did the phony maiden pass by?
Did the terrifying old ladies of the green salon pass?
And you, magistrates, shake your bell, darling magistrates, shake it furiously
now that the elevator has descended.
Does it want to ascend with me?
Truly I have such courage
I would like to accompany those who'll go out tonight.
But they refuse to tell us where we'll be judged,
yes, the lion knows where his deposition will be heard,
but he is the undisputed king of the jungle,
and I mean, We, the residents of this hotel
with the tunnel that circulates without pity.
It is remarkable, the voices can't be heard beyond the first floor,
and I know that there are people awaiting certain calls…
They say the lion will be absolved.
Meanwhile let's take a walk around the neighborhood.

Do you notice perhaps the trees or, better yet, the tongue of the tunnel
sticking out the window?
I'm not sure it's really a chain.
Suddenly a stentorian voice announces:

¡Absuelto el león! Todos se estremecen.
Alma mía, será mejor que entres en el túnel.
Con gran estupefacción del tribunal el león acaba de suicidarse.

II.

No, si yo circulo, si hago leves inclinaciones a derecha e izquierda,
si me abro la camisa y muestro el pecho,
no, no es esa la verdadera causa,
es, más bien, mi resistencia, mi horror magnífico a no ser juzgado
a las seis de la tarde.
De cualquier modo seré emplazado,
bajaré entre grandes calores hasta el piso bajo.
Entonces no podrás invitarme porque el interrogatorio será muy largo.
Hay muchos casos,
y no sé por qué motivo se me quiere juzgar precisamente
a las seis de la tarde.
Todos saben que soy un recién llegado.
Ni siquiera conozco el corredor que lleva a la cocina,
ni las dos paredes altas que se unen a las doce del día
para que mueran las ratas que infectan el patio de las aguaspluviales.

Sabes, alma mía, que soy un simple mortal,
que me gusta ser el matasellos de la gran ciudad
y me gusta la banda de música en el parque.

Pero sí, he de protestar,
hablaré con el homúnculo del ascensor,
voy a gritar.
¡Oh, qué extraño!,
cada vez que lanzo un grito el túnel palidece,
se pone una rosa fúnebre y dice:
¡Ay de mí!

III
Del hotel una dorada rodilla empieza la genuflexión,
atrayendo todo lo que es helado documento a las seis de la tarde,

The lion's absolved! There's a huge commotion.
Dear soul, it's best if you enter the tunnel.
The tribunal is dumbfounded: the lion has just committed suicide.

II.

No, if I circle about, moving slightly left and right,
if I open my shirt and bare my chest,
no, that is not the real cause,
it is, rather, my resistance, my grand horror of being judged
at six in the afternoon.
In any event I'll be summoned,
I'll descend through great heat to the lower floor.
Then you won't be able to invite me because it will be a very long interrogation.
There are many cases,
and I don't quite know why I'm being judged
at six in the afternoon.
Everyone knows I'm a recent arrival.
I'm not even familiar with the hallway leading to the kitchen,
or the two high walls that come together at noon
to kill the rats that infest the patio of the rain waters.

You know, dear soul, that I'm a simple man,
I like being the great city's postmark
and I like the band playing music in the park.

But yes, I must protest,
I'll speak with the homunculus in the elevator,
and I'll scream,
How strange!
Each time I shout the tunnel grows pale,
it wears a funeral rose and says,
Pity me!

III.
In the hotel, a golden knee begins the genuflection,
attracting all that is an icy document at six in the afternoon,

todo cuanto puede ser más tarde o antes ardiente,
pero que en ese momento de las seis es la congelación del sol.

¿Puede aún afirmarse que es una cadena?
Veo cómo el gran animal salta,
sus eslabones se refugian en el seno de las damas,
veo cómo las túnicas del tribunal se mueven al compás de sus resoplidos,

su lengua exige la saliva de todos,
su lengua, muy dignamente, asperja aquí y allá.

Contra paredes amarillas, contra epitafios que no se ven, repta,
descifra los mensajes dejados por el polvo de los zapatos en los mosaicos,
nadie escapa al brillo de su lengua,
nadie resiste su perfecta movilidad,
unos a otros se observan con la mirada propia de los actores en escena
para comunicarse que todos son al fin la gran lengua.
Y yo también, sí, yo ahora me muevo por el salón con velocidad pasmosa,
soy la gran lengua,
todo cuanto choca contra mi púrpura se hace púrpura cruzada de férreas astas,
pero ya no es las seis de la tarde. He sido sentenciado.

Alguien me precede en este salón que es como un plato de sangre,
un plato de sangre con una cabeza de buey sobrenadando,
una cabeza de buey para alimentar tu lengua, para apagar tu sed.
¡Qué risa, mi lengua sobre el mismo bocado!
El giro eterno y esas aves que salen de sus papilas,
esas grandes aves remontando el vuelo hasta perderse en la cola del sol,
esas grandes aves encima del silencio.

1944

all that could be burning after or before,
but at six o'clock is a frozen sun.

Can it still be affirmed that it's a chain?
I see how the large animal jumps,
its links seek refuge in the breast of ladies,
I see how the tunics of the magistrates move to the beat of their panting,

their tongues demand everyone's saliva,
with great dignity their tongues spray here and there.

Against yellow walls, against epitaphs no one sees, the tongues crawl,
they decipher messages left by the dust of shoes on the tiles,
no one escapes the sheen of their tongues,
no one resists their perfect mobility,
they observe one another with the look of actors on stage
to say that they're all, finally, one great tongue.
And I too, yes, I now move through the hall with blinding speed,
I am the great tongue,
everything that comes against my purple becomes purple run through by steel horns,
but it is no longer six in the afternoon. I have been sentenced.

Someone precedes me in the hall like a plate of blood,
a plate of blood with an ox head in the center,
an ox head to feed your tongue, to quench your thirst.
How funny, my tongue going for the same morsel!
The eternal circle and those birds coming out of its taste buds,
those huge birds taking flight until they are lost in the sun's tail,
those huge birds over the silence.

1944

Poema para la poesía

Avanza el mar y quiere el blondo pez ensimismarse lentamente,
ensimismarse sin la menor espuma en medio de estos peces agrupados
junto a una estatua combatida ferozmente por la única ola
que viene de noche a morder su rostro impasible.
No, yo no quiero entrar por esa puerta:
pequeñas conchas y fúnebres caballos haciendo la vida,
sin la menor ondulación, sin el menor simulacro de mascarada,
todo claramente como si un sueño fuera a producirse.

Así vamos en la deteriorada vértebra a salir al mar,
notablemente arrugado sin mi amoroso deseo,
sin los castillos donde lame un perro.
Estos animales venían de muy lejos,
sin traer en sus patas el postrer deseo de las damas.
Entra el cartero y me entrega la carta recibida en el sueño,
esas tarjetas con la pálida Rosamunda parada sobre sus senos.
Imposible pensar la vida a través de una lluvia matemática.

Leves pisadas en el fango espeso de la copa del gigante.
No me detengo, no me asombro,
la sorpresa llega en el vientre de un pez.
Tu paz y las desesperadas llamadas del amor,
violar las túnicas dejando el cuerpo intacto.
Dioses, dioses, palabras siempre yacentes
para que nadie interrumpa su alta majestad.
Estoy impulsando este poema y esto puede matarme.

Perro, ven perro, perro sin un ladrido, desoladamente canino.
Qué flores arrojar o qué gavetas.
Todo va a comenzar. Tengo una cáscara.

Los pergaminos, los rollos y las indefinibles técnicas del hombre,
como si envolver, plegar fuera el objeto de esa garra.

Poem for Poetry

The sea advances and the blond fish wants to self-obsess
slowly, without any foam in the midst of this group of fish
surrounding a statue beaten fiercely by the only wave
that comes at night to bite its expressionless face.
No, I don't want to enter that door:
small shells and funereal horses living their lives
without any waves, without any simulacrum of a masquerade,
all clear as if a dream were about to happen.

And so I go on the deteriorated vertebra moving out to sea,
notably wrinkled without my desire for love,
without the castles where a dog is licking.
These animals came from very far
without bringing on their legs the last desire of the ladies.
The mailman enters and gives me a letter received in the dream,
those cards with pale Rosemond standing on her breasts.
Impossible to imagine life through a mathematical rain.

Light steps in the thick mud of the giant's cup.
I don't stop, I'm not surprised,
surprise comes in the belly of a fish.
Your peace and the desperate calls for love,
raping tunics and leaving the body intact.
Gods, gods, words always in wait
so that no one interrupts their high majesty.
I am driving the poem and this can kill me.

Dog, come dog, dog without a bark, desolate canine.
What roses to hurl, what dresser drawers.
Everything is about to begin. I have a rind.

The parchments, the rolls, the undefinable techniques of man,
as if wrapping or folding were the purpose of that claw.

No salen por la ventana las llamas y el humo no indica
que el Papa se llamará Impiedad.

Las mujeres avanzan con un pie en la boca,
mi caracol resonador revienta la cabeza de la comedianta.
Todo el mundo ha olvidado su papel:
¡Qué alegría no representar esta noche!
El público protesta y comienza el coito de las sirenas.

Ese seno…qué indescriptible viaje me ha contado,
era algo así como si un caballo y la creación poética se reuniesen en un jardín.
¡Oh, qué furia!, yerbas pisoteadas, y la mejor flor interrumpiendo su perfume.

¡Qué furia, qué dolor! Estas espumas y el punzante recuerdo
de aquellos pies cercenados en lo mejor de la danza.
Un viaje indescriptible de la soledad de los danzantes,
con la soledad y la melodía extraviada de una orquesta.
Puedo perecer y encontrar un amigo.

Esta cabeza, sus llamas, sus cabellos empapados de melancolía,
las primeras venas y el hueso donde llamo para distraerme.

El pantano del espíritu…
No, yo no quiero, no quiero.

¡Oh, perro mío, orina más y más con tu pata levantada!
El frío mortal de estos países cálidos:
usted llama, nadie responde,
las bocas apretadas, la sangre en la planta de los pies
y el corazón como un antiguo salón abandonado.
Necesito el amor, las toallas, los monumentos.
Vanas lamentaciones. Un pulpo suelta su tinta y se pone a llorar.
No, yo no quiero entrar,
y el mundo me basta.
¿Para qué todo ese vano aparato? ¿Para qué ese juez?

Flames are not coming out the window and the smoke doesn't signal
that the Pope will be named Impious.

The women advance with a foot in their mouth,
my resonant conch will burst the head of the comedienne.
Everyone has forgotten their role:
What joy not to go on stage tonight!
The public protests and the coitus of mermaids begins.

That breast…what an indescribable voyage it has told me,
as if a horse and poetic creation came together in a garden.
Oh what fury! Trampled grass and the best flower interrupting its perfume.

What fury, what sorrow! These foams and the piercing memory
of those feet amputated during the best part of the dance.
An indescribable trip about the solitude of the dancers,
with the solitude and the lost melody of an orchestra.
I can die and find a friend.

This head, its flames, its hair soaked with melancholy,
the first veins and the bone where I call for the sake of distraction.

The swamp of the spirit…
No, I refuse, I refuse.

O dog of mine, piss all you can with your leg raised.
The deadly cold of these warm countries:
you call, no one answers,
tight mouths, blood on the soles of the feet
and the heart like an old, abandoned ballroom.
I need love, towels, monuments.
Vain lamentations. An octopus sprays its ink and starts to cry.
No, I don't want to enter
and the world is enough.
Why all that vain machinery, why that judge?

No, yo no quiero entrar,
tejo las últimas guirnaldas y tiendo la vista al horizonte.
¿Y si de pronto me quedo muerto en medio de la calle?
¿Y si de pronto comprendo el amor?
¿Y si súbitamente me dibujo?
¡Oh, no, qué hiriente melodía, qué ladrido!
¿Concretamente puedo enumerarme?

Pero de súbito me quedo sin los símbolos:
sabe usted, un mundo enteramente inerte:
me presentan un cuadro. Nada.
Me entregan a la música. Nada.
Me leen un poema. Nada.
¿Quién irá a perecer?

¡Oh, piedras, muchas piedras, rocas, cubridme!
Un dedo en el agua puede comunicar el frío a todo el cuerpo.
Sería inútil saber que Filemón y Baucis...
Inútilmente llegas a decirme que Leonardo...
No –te digo–, y casi me sonrío.
¡Qué miseria!: pájaro, oiseau, bird, uccello...
Es para golpearse la cabeza,
es para no existir.
Babel, Babel, Babel, pero nadie responde.

El viento acompaña esta amarga costumbre que es hablar,
su médula corriendo enloquecida por las cámaras de la flauta
como si la última palabra fuera a ser pronunciada
o como si el gato frente a mí dijera:
«Hoy hará un hermoso día...».
Usted se inclina, yo me inclino, no hablamos media palabra,
usted me clava un puñal, yo robo un reloj de oro.
No, no hay juez,
el pelotón de fusilamiento ofrece al reo una merienda.
El mundo como hechos sin calificativos.
¿Y aquella frase?

No, I don't want to enter.
I weave the last garlands and look at the horizon.
What if suddenly I fall dead in the middle of the street?
What if suddenly I understand love?
What if suddenly I draw myself?
Oh no, what a hurtful melody, what a bark!
Can I count myself concretely?

But suddenly I remain without symbols:
you know, a totally inert world:
they show me a painting. Nothing.
They offer me music. Nothing.
They read me a poem. Nothing.
Who is going to die?

Oh, stones, many stones, rocks, cover me!
One finger in the water can make the whole body cold.
It would be useless to know that Philemon and Baucis…
Uselessly you come to tell me that Leonardo…
No, I tell you, and I almost smile.
What misery! pájaro, oiseau, bird, uccello…
It's enough to beat yourself on the head
so as not to exist.
Babel, Babel, Babel, but no one answers.

The wind accompanies the bitter habit of talking,
its medulla racing madly down the chambers of a flute
as if the last word were about to be spoken
or as if the cat before me were to say:
"Today will be a beautiful day."
You lean, I lean, we don't speak a single word.
you stick a knife into me, I steal a gold watch.
No, there's no judge,
the firing squad offers a snack to the condemned man.
The world as facts without qualification.
And that phrase?

«Un corcho en medio de las hirvientes aguas»...
No queda una sola fotografía del Partenón ni tampoco del Vaticano,
nada queda sino el Amor.
¡Oh, perro, perro mío, aúlla,
ofréceme un poema de aullidos, concédeme esta gracia extrema,
tú mismo lo leerás,
mientras yo quemo los demás poemas!

1944

"A cork in the midst of boiling waters..."
There isn't a single photograph of the Parthenon or the Vatican,
nothing remains except Love.
Oh, dog, dog of mine, howl,
offer me a poem of howls, concede me this great favor,
you will read it yourself,
while I burn the rest of the poems!

1944

Yo lo veo

Mejor sería que la muerte alzara
esa corona de tu vida,
así la pesaría,
y en la frente donde la luna mete sus reflejos
esplendería hasta vencer su propia rigidez.

Estás desnudo
como si los días resbalaran sin horas por tu cuerpo,
como si un veloz animal interpusiera su carrera
entre el reposo y los recuerdos.

Ya el día empieza su ascensión,
y tú terminas en el abrupto pico de la inercia.
Me estás llamando como si en mi oído
cayeran una a una las mortajas impenetrables de la destrucción.

Y yo también te llamo destruido,
alcanzo tus contornos,
te inflamo con esos soles de mi condolencia,
te meto en tu caja de lamentos,
me alcanza tu pavor y rompo el aire
con vibraciones de su impedimento,
te veo por los aires como un astro muerto
deshaciéndose en lunas enfriadas,
te veo con tus zapatos y tu perfección.

1945

I See It

Better death raise
the crown of your life
to weigh it,
and on the forehead where the moon hides its reflection
death will overcome its own severity with splendor.

You are naked,
as if the hourless days slid down your body,
as if a fleeting animal raced
between rest and memory.

Day now begins its ascent
and you end up in the sudden beak of inertia.
You call me as if the impregnable shrouds
of destruction dropped on my ear one by one.

And I too label you destroyed,
I reach your outskirts,
I set fire to you with the suns of my condolence,
I place you in a box of laments,
your fear reaches me and I wreck the air
with the vibrations of its impediment.
I see you in the air like a dead star
shattering into cold moons,
I see you with your shoes and your perfection.

1945

Tesis del gabinete azul

Puede el gabinete azul brindarme su espacio
y sus pausas enguantadas brindarme puede;
puede también brindarme su lecho,
reducido por el horror que provoca el visitante de las dos en punto.

Puede revolverse y abatir sus columnas
y hacer pasar el terremoto del canalla por sus mármoles.
Esto y más puede por su existencia de gabinete azul,
ligeramente pintado de azul por el guardabosques.

Pero no podrá jamás hacer de mí un gabinete azul
enclavado en el césped del señor del castillo,
con su cordón de seda estrangulando los días,
mientras camina hacia atrás para no penetrar en su fastuoso recinto.

Jamás el gabinete azul podrá entrar en mi espacio
ni yo le brindaré mis mortales esperas
de gabinete azul dispuesto a todo.
No podrá jamás, y esto lo conmueve de tal modo
que me exige transformarme en gabinete azul
y aguardar sus entradas de rey que lleva un ave.

No siendo esto posible entonces entro en él,
entonces a sus pausas enguantadas me entrego,
y lo estrangulo con el cordón de seda de los días.
Entonces al dejarlo desplomado en sus mármoles
puede el gabinete azul salir y abandonarme
como si hubiera entrado en mí a fin de horrorizarme.

1945

Thesis of the Blue Cabinet

The blue cabinet can offer me its space
and offer its gloved pauses as well;
offer me its bed, diminished by the terror
the prompt visitor provokes at two o'clock.

It can shake itself and tear down its columns
and allow the earthquake of the miser to pass through its marbles.
It can do this and more by simply being a blue cabinet,
lightly painted by the forester.

But it'll never turn me into a blue cabinet
placed in the lawn of the lord's manor
with its silk cord strangling the days
as it walks backward to avoid entering the lavish domain.

Never can the blue cabinet enter my space,
nor will I offer it my mortal hopes
of a blue cabinet ready for anything.
It never can, and this moves it so
that it demands I turn into a blue cabinet
and thus await its royal entrances like a bird.

Since this is not possible I enter into it,
then surrender to its gloved pauses
and strangle it with the silk cord of days.
Then when I leave it collapsed on its marbles
the blue cabinet can go and abandon me
as if it had entered me in order to terrorize me.

1945

Un bamboleo frenético

No pienses…
Date duro en la cabeza,
martillea, entra y sal sin descanso,
persigue el objeto pérfido,
muévete entre sueños,
y… golpea, siempre golpea,
sin solemnidad y sin belleza.
No hacen falta en esta hora en que caes para siempre.
Ajeno al pensamiento,
cae de los pies a la cabeza
golpeando y golpeando este momento mortal.
Audaz, cae.
Sueña contigo en la tarde
engañosamente se presenta como el confín
de la promesa que miente con labios dorados.
Anoche te debatías en el fango,
te encharcabas en ese baile espeso
anunciador del frío de la tumba.
Golpea y golpea hasta romper.
Es la hora de la decisión.
Convoca a los sonidos para que no cese la música
de solo y solo.
Solo, con golpes y genuflexiones,
la sangre y nuevos golpes.
¿Quién se queja a esta hora
en que solo y solo pasa la existencia?
Húndete en los golpes
y bebe tu propia proscripción.
Solo y solo en un dedo parado,
tu último llamamiento a la catástrofe.
Desarticulado de todo, antes que todo y…
siempre solo,
con heridas, con un solo de muecas.

A Frenetic Sway

Don't think. . .
Hit your head hard,
hammer it, go in and out without a break,
follow the deceitful object,
move among your dreams,
and hit, always hit
without solemnity or beauty.
They are useless to you now when you are forever falling.
Foreign to thought,
fall from the feet to the head,
hitting again and again this deadly moment.
Brazen, fall.
Dream about yourself in the afternoon
foolishly presented like the borders of a promise
that tells lies with golden lips.
Last night you argued with yourself in the mud,
you were stuck in that thick dance
announcing the cold of the grave.
Hit and hit again until you break.
It is time for a decision.
Call together your sounds so that the music doesn't stop
from solo to solo.
Alone, with blows and genuflections,
blood and more blows.
Who complains at this hour
when existence passes from solo to solo?
Lean into the blows
and drink your own prohibition.
Solo and alone with one finger standing,
your last call to catastrophe.
Disconnected from everything, before everything and. . .
always alone,
with wounds, with a solo of gestures.

Golpea si quieres que la descomposición te visite,
no desoigas la voz, sigue esa calle y…
con solo y solo baila hasta destriparte.
Que la soledad sea tu solo de moscas y…
¡cataplum! ¡Al hoyo!
Que la caja retumbe en tus oídos:
«Aparta la perfección agazapada
el colgajo de serenidad».
Solo entre acompañados
rueda en la rueda de los solos,
en solo de solo con tu solo,
solo nimbado yo te llamo
para zamparte solo y solo en la noche giratoria.

1961

Hit if you want decomposition to visit,
don't ignore the voice, follow that street and. . .
with solo and solo dance till you drop.
Let solitude be your solo of flies and…
Ka-boom! Into the hole!
Let the coffin echo in your ears:
"Sly perfection pulls away
the cover of serenity."
Alone among couples
round in the round of solos,
in a solo of solos with your solo,
solo with aura I call you
to devour you alone, alone in the whirling night.

1961

Sin embargo…

Después que me lo dijeron
perdí el sueño, perdí el habla;
yo siempre voy a ese bar
a darme unos cuantos tragos.
Si no me pasó a mí
es porque llegué tarde.
El tipo se colocó
en el sitio en que me paro
cuando tomo mi cerveza
pensando en la musarañas.
La bala le dio en el pecho
—de casualidad la bala—
mientras el disco decía
que la vida es un carajo.
Después, como hay que vivir,
me fui al cine a anestesiarme;
todo terminaba bien.
Sin embargo, sin embargo…

1962

Nevertheless

After they told me
I lost my sleep, I lost my speech;
I always go to that bar
to have a few drinks.
If it didn't happen to me
it's because I arrived late.
The guy was standing
in the same spot
where I drink my beer
thinking about nothing in particular.
The bullet hit him in the chest
—by chance, the bullet—
while the juke box said
life is a bitch.
Then, since one must live,
I went to the movies to numb myself;
everything ended well.
Nevertheless, nevertheless...

1962

El jardín

Un jardín me ha construido el sueño
para que en él yo sueñe la realidad;
allí los muertos, los vivos, los ausentes
conversan entre sí animadamente:
a mi difunta madre yo le he oído
quejarse de las frutas del mal año,
y decirle a mi padre que yo soy
un niño desterrado de su amor.

De pronto ha aparecido Robespierre
sentado en su carreta del patíbulo
vendiendo una cabeza con gusanos
mientras grita: ¡Manzanas coloradas!
Mi padre pide una, y él le dice:
¿Cuál prefieres? ¿La de Dantón?
¿La de María Antonieta?
Pero mi madre viendo una cabeza
en donde por las cuencas de los ojos
asomaban dos uvas temblorosas,
la eligió, y Robespierre le dijo:
Es para mí un honor que usted me coma.

Lo que leí en los inciertos libros
ahora lo veo señaladamente:
Nerval se va a ahorcar en la Vieille Lanterne,
Zenea se dispone a ser fusilado,
Casal en su hemoptisis se consume,
y en Dos Ríos Martí la patria funda.

De Henry James los niños misteriosos
se acercan a su aya desencarnada
para confiarle que ellos están viendo
un hombre vivo en lo alto de la torre.

The Garden

Sleep has made me a garden
so that in it I can dream reality;
there the dead, the living, the absent
talk eagerly among themselves:
I've heard my dead mother
complain about the fruits of that bad year
and tell my father that I am
a child banned from her love.

Suddenly Robespierre appears
seated in his gallows wagon
selling a head full of worms
while screaming: Red apples!
My father asks for one and Robespierre tells him:
Which would you like? Danton's,
Marie Antoinette's?
My mother, seeing one
with two trembling grapes in the eye sockets,
picked it and Robespierre said,
It's an honor that you eat me.

What I read in uncertain books
I now see clearly:
Nerval is going to hang himself on the Vieille Lanterne,
Zenea gets ready for the firing squad,
Casal is consumed by hemoptysis,
and at Dos Ríos Martí founds the nation.

Out of Henry James the mysterious children
approach their bodiless nanny
to let her know that they've seen
a live man atop the tower.
Smiling she nods and takes a finger

Sonriendo ella asiente y pone un dedo
sobre sus labios como diciéndoles:
Todo es posible en el reino de la muerte.

Aún no salido de mi asombro escucho
de Carlos Marx la voz tronitonante:
Aunque quieras los ángeles no existen.
Vas caminando por una estrecha calle,
o por el ancho mar o el aire surcas
y no hay ángeles que choquen con tu vista;
sólo hay seres humanos y animales
que mueven como pueden su existencia.
Tu pensamiento debes concentrar en ellos,
en una esquina abandonar la fantasía,
dejarla ciega, que se estrelle sola,
y tú decir con convicción profunda:
Somos materialistas convencidos.

Ya no tienen cabida en este mundo
las locas invenciones de la mente,
las gorgonas se han ido para siempre,
en los océanos no hay buques fantasmas,
y aquel que caminó sobre las aguas
se ha perdido en el lago de los Quantas.

En el teatro de los idealistas,
Hegel (si lo pudieras ver), menos que ambiguo
está, olímpico, detrás de la cortina,
sentado entre la tesis y la antítesis.
No hay público para escuchar su verbo:
toda la fenomenología del espíritu
es un sólido bloque de materia
contra el que las mónadas se estrellan.

Tú estás aquí, en este jardín,
estás bien muerto y, sin embargo,

to her lips as if to say:
Everything is possible in the kingdom of death.

I haven't gotten over my surprise
when I hear Karl Marx's thunderous voice:
no matter how much you want them, angels don't exist.
You walk down a narrow street
or by the wide sea to feel the breeze
and there are no angels crossing your path;
only humans and animals
that move their being as best they can.
You should concentrate your thoughts on them
and abandon fantasy at the corner,
leave her blind, let her fall apart by herself,
then you can say with deep conviction:
We are confirmed materialists.

There's no room in this world
for the crazy inventions of the mind,
gorgons have left us forever,
there are no ghost ships on the ocean,
and he who walked on water
is lost in the quantum lake.

In the theater of the idealists,
Hegel (if you could see him) is less than ambiguous,
more than Olympic, and sits behind the curtain
between thesis and antithesis.
There's no public to listen to his words:
all of the phenomenology of the spirit
is a solid block of matter
against which monads crash.

You are here, in this garden,
fully dead, and yet,
I hear your voice speaking about matter.

oigo tu voz hablando de materia.
Y Marx contesta: No soy yo el que te habla,
eres tú el que me sueña.
Estás vivo y estás soñando
que yo te hablo de la materia,
de la que tu sueño es una parte.

Dime, le imploro, ¿el que está muerto
en su hoyo es mecido por el sueño?
Yo he muerto, dice Marx, y tú aún eres
materia viviente. Hablo por tu mente,
y en nada soy mecido, al menos que tú digas
que yo me estoy meciendo.

Desde un púlpito con blancos espectrales
la voz de un sacerdote cae helada:
Los designios de Dios son insondables,
y aunque las naves viajen a la Luna
en tierra nos quedamos con el tiempo.
Sólo el espíritu puede redimirnos
de tal arena aciaga, y esta envoltura corporal
convertirla en gusanos, y que surja
la eternidad empapándose en la Muerte.

Muy lindas tus palabras –dice Marx–,
pero las naves viajan a la Luna,
y en tu cabeza tus ángeles vuelan
como las moscas sobre el cadáver.
Enseña a tu rebaño que el poema,
en las casas mentales, siempre ocupa
un lugar irrisorio, y diles
que vivimos en un mundo
donde soñar es como estar ya muertos.

1965

And Marx answers: It's not I who speaks to you,
it's your dream of me.
You are alive and you are dreaming
that I speak to you of matter,
of which your dream is a part.

Tell me, I implore you, he who is dead
and in his hole, is he rocked by sleep?
I have died, says Marx, and you are still
living matter. I speak through your mind,
and am not at all rocked, unless you mean
that I am rocking myself.

From a pulpit with white ghosts
the voice of a priest drops icily:
The designs of God are unknown,
and even if ships fly to the Moon,
on earth we are subject to time.
Only the spirit can redeem us
from nefarious dust, and turn
this bodily vessel into worms,
and let eternity surge soaked with death.

Such pretty words, says Marx,
but ships travel to the Moon
and in your head angels fly
like flies over a corpse.
Teach your flock that the poem
always occupies a ridiculous place
in the houses of the mind and tell them
that we live in a world
where dreaming is akin to being dead.

1965

Poema para ser dicho en medio de un gran silencio

¿Será que van a matar?
¿Será que con el cuchillo más grande traspasarán el corazón?
¿Y con el bisturí más afilado vaciarán los ojos?
¿Y con el cortahierros más hierros romperán el cráneo?
¿Y con el martillo más martillo machacarán los huesos?

¿Será que en la mesa erótica
–mesa carnal y mesa-amor–,
amor mío, tú y yo
en el ser sobrecogidos,
una noche tu corazón
habló cuando estabas bajo mi sangre?
¿Será lo mismo que fue cuando siendo,
cuando siendo un juramento, y más que eso,
tu palabra, tu palabra sangró,
empapada en el perfume tenue de los besos,
para no negar, para ser uno en lo indiviso?
¿Y se cree tan ciegamente,
tan ciegamente que todos los soles se apagan para siempre
mientras el alma navega por lo oscuro?
¿Será que nunca hubo alma a pesar de las músicas que olamos?
¿Alma que no fue aunque alma fueras tan sólo un instante?
¿Te acuerdas de ese instante en que alma siendo me adoraste,
y entonces tu propio monstruo sobrevino
para llevarte al donde siendo fuiste?

¿Será que después que no seas,
cuando no ser es sólo montón de besos disecados,
serás no siendo, pero siendo amor?

1967

Poem to be Said in the Midst of a Great Silence

Can it be they are going to kill?
Will they pierce the heart with a huge knife?
And with the sharpest scalpel empty the eyes?
And with the steeliest chisel break the skull?
And with the most hammer of hammers crush the bones?

Can it be that on the erotic table
–table of sex, table of love–
my love, you and I,
being startled one night
your heart spoke
when you were under my blood?
Can it be the same as it was
when it was an oath, and even more so,
your word, your word bled,
soaked by the soft perfume of kisses,
so as not to deny, to be one indivisible?
And can it be so blindly believed,
so blindly, that all the suns go dark forever
while the soul travels in darkness?
Can it be there never was a soul despite the waves of music we made?
Soul that never was though soul you might be for an instant?
Remember that instant when you were a soul and adored me,
and then your own monster came suddenly
to take you to the place where being you were?

Can it be that after you are no longer,
when not being is merely a mound of dried out kisses,
you will be by not being, instead being love?

1967

En el gato tuerto

En el Gato Tuerto no hay gatos.
En el Gato Tuerto hay gente,
con ojos como prismáticos,
con bocas como ventosas,
con manos como tentáculos,
con pies como detectores.

En el Gato Tuerto
hay una noche dentro de la noche,
con una luna que sale para algunos,
un sol que brilla para otros
y un gallo que canta para todos.

En el Gato Tuerto
hay el asiento de la felicidad,
hay el asiento de la desdicha,
y hay también el horrendo asiento de la espera.

En el Gato Tuerto,
¿me atreveré a decirlo?,
hay un pañuelo para enjugar la lágrimas,
y hay igualmente
—casi no me atrevo—
un espejo para mirarse cara a cara.

En el Gato Tuerto
una noche se dieron el sí dos amantes,
y en el Gato Tuerto
otra noche mataron lo que amaban.
En el Gato Tuerto
hay un momento de expectación
cuando el amante imaginario
hace su aparición.

At the One-Eyed Cat

At the One-Eyed Cat there are no cats.
At the One-Eyed Cat there are people
with eyes like prisms,
with mouths like suckers,
with hands like tentacles,
with feet like detectors.

At the One-Eyed Cat
there is a night inside the night,
with a moon that rises for some,
a sun that shines for others
and a rooster that crows for all.

At the One-Eyed Cat
there is the seat of happiness,
there is the seat of misery,
and there is also the terrible seat of waiting.

At the One-Eyed Cat,
dare I say it?,
there is a handkerchief to soak up tears
and there is likewise–
I almost don't dare–
a mirror to look oneself in the face.

At the One-Eyed Cat
one night two lovers said yes,
and at the One-Eyed Cat,
another night they killed their love.
At the One-Eyed Cat
there is a moment of anticipation
when the imaginary lover
makes his entrance.

Mira amorosamente y dice:
«¡Soy de quien me espera!»,
y entonces el *feeling* llega al corazón,
en el Gato Tuerto con Revolución.

1967

He looks lovingly around and says:
"I belong to whoever waits for me."
and then a feeling reaches the heart,
at the One-Eyed Cat and Revolution.

1967

de Una broma colosal

from A Colossal Joke

Lo de menos

Lo de menos:
que tú no me ames,
y lo de más:
que soy el que te ama.
Es mi hermosa ventaja,
y no como piensan los bobos,
mi triste ventaja.
Soy tu cosa,
el piano que estás tocando,
y mientras tocas, te dices:
«Un piano es solo un piano».
Pero también,
casi con amargura:
«¡Qué enamorado está de mí!».
Quisieras arañarme
–y comprendo tu rabia–:
no estás en disposición de acariciarme,
en tanto que yo,
con la soberanía del amor,
te acaricio con la mirada.
Y tu alma, como un vampiro,
bebe la sangre de mi alma:
cada gota es la copa del lento veneno
que se administran los indiferentes.
Roto, exangüe,
incorpóreo, expirante
puedo decirte:
No me ames.

1967

The Least of It

The least of it:
that you don't love me,
and the most of it:
that I'm the one who loves you.
It is my beautiful advantage,
and not as fools think,
my sorrowful advantage.
I am your thing,
the piano you play,
and while you play, you say,
"A piano is only a piano."
But also,
with bitterness almost,
"How he's fallen for me!"
You'd like to scratch me
—and I understand your rage:
you're in no mood to touch me,
while I,
sovereign in my love,
touch you with my gaze.
And your soul, like a vampire,
drinks my soul's blood:
each drop is the cup of slow poison
the indifferent drink.
Broken, out of blood,
bodiless, expiring
I can tell you:
Don't love me.

1967

Si muero en la carretera

I.

Si muero en la carretera no me pongan flores.
Si en la carretera muero no me pongan flores.
En la carretera no me pongan flores si muero.
No me pongan si muero flores en la carretera.
No me pongan en la carretera flores si muero.
No flores en la carretera si muero me pongan.
No flores en la carretera me pongan si muero.
Si muero no flores en la carretera me pongan.
Si flores me muero en la carretera no me pongan.
Flores si muero no en la carretera me pongan.
Si flores muero pongan en me la no carretera.
Flores si pongan muero me en no la carretera.
Muero si pongan flores la en me no carretera.
La muero en si pongan no me carretera.
Si flores muero pongan en me la no carretera.
Flores si pongan muero me en no la carretera.
Si muero en las flores no me pongan en la carretera.
Si flores muero no me pongan en la carretera.
Si en la carretera flores no me pongan si muero.
Si en el muero no me pongan en la carretera flores.

II

Voy en cacharrito, en una cafetera,
yo voy por la carretera;
yo voy, voy yendo por la carretera.
Yo voy a un jardín de flores que está por la carretera,
yo voy en un cacharrito, en una cafetera,
voy a comprarle flores a mis muertos,
pero no me pongan flores si muero en la carretera.

III.

Si muero en la carretera me entierran en el jardín

If I Die on the Highway

I.

If I die on the highway leave me no flowers.
If on the highway I die leave me no flowers.
On the highway leave me no flowers if I die.
Leave me if I die no flowers on the highway.
Leave me on the highway no flowers if I die.
No flowers on the highway if I die leave me.
No flowers on the highway leave me if I die.
If I die no flowers on the highway leave me.
If flowers I die on the highway no leave me.
Flowers if I die no on the highway leave me.
If flowers I die leave on me the no highway.
Flowers if leave I die me on no the highway.
I die if leave flowers the on me no highway.
The I die on if leave no me highway.
If flowers I die leave on me the no highway.
Flowers if leave I die me on no the highway.
If I die on the flowers leave me no on the highway.
If flowers I die leave me no on the highway.
If on the highway flowers leave me no if I die.
If on the I die leave me no on the highway flowers.

II.

I'm driving a little clunker, a coffee pot,
I'm driving down the highway;
I'm going, going, gone on the highway.
I'm going to a flower garden near the highway,
I'm going in a little clunker, a coffee pot,
I'm going to buy flowers in honor of the dead,
but leave me no flowers if I die on the highway.

III.

If I die on the highway bury me in the garden

que está por la carretera, pero no me pongan flores,

cuando uno tiene su fin yendo por la carretera
a uno no le ponen flores de ese ni de otro jardín.

IV.

Si muero, si no muero,
si muero porque no muero
si no muero porque muero.
Si muero en la carretera.
Si no muero pero en la carretera si muero.
Si muero porque no muero en la carretera.
Si no muero porque muero en la carretera,
no me pongan f, no me pongan l, no me pongan o,
no me pongan r, no me pongan e, no me pongan s,
no me pongan flo, no me pongan res,
si muero en la c.

1970

near the highway, but leave me no flowers,

when you meet your end going down the highway,
no one leaves flowers from that or any other garden.

IV.

If I die, if I don't die,
if I die because I don't die,
if I don't die because I die.
If I die on the highway.
If I don't die but on the highway if I die.
If I die because I don't die on the highway.
If I don't die because I die on the highway,
leave me no f, leave me no l, leave me no o
leave me no w, leave me no e, leave me no r, leave me no s,
leave me no flow, leave me no ers,
if I die on the h.

1970

Bueno, digamos

A Lezama

Bueno, digamos que hemos vivido,
no ciertamente –aunque sería elegante–
como los griegos de la polis radiante,
sino parecidos a estatuas kriselefantinas,
y con un asomo de esteatopigia.
Hemos vivido en una isla,
quizá no como quisimos,
pero como pudimos.
Aun así derribamos algunos templos,
y levantamos otros
que tal vez perduren
o sean a su tiempo derribados.
Hemos escrito infatigablemente,
soñado lo suficiente
para penetrar la realidad.
Alzamos diques
contra la idolatría y lo crepuscular.
Hemos rendido culto al sol
y, algo aún más esplendoroso,
luchamos para ser esplendentes.
Ahora, callados por un rato,
oímos ciudades deshechas en polvo,
arder en pavesas insignes manuscritos,
y el lento, cotidiano gotear del odio.
Mas, es sólo una pausa en nuestro devenir.
Pronto nos pondremos a conversar.
No encima de las ruinas, sino del recuerdo,
porque fíjate: son ingrávidos
y nosotros ahora empezamos.

1972

Well, Let Us Say

for Lezama

Well, let us say that we've lived,
clearly not—though that would be elegant—
as the Greeks of the radiant polis,
but rather like chryselephantine statues
with a slight case of steatopygia.
We have lived on an island,
perhaps not as we wanted
but as we could.
Even so we tore down some temples
and raised others
that might perhaps last
or themselves be torn down in due time.
We have written without rest,
dreamed enough
to penetrate reality.
We built dikes
against idolatry and decay.
We have worshipped the sun
and in our splendor,
we struggled to shine with our own light.
Now, silenced for a while,
we hear of cities turned to dust,
priceless manuscripts burned to ashes,
and the slow, daily drip of hatred.
But this is a mere pause in our evolution.
Soon we'll converse,
not atop ruins but atop memory
because, take note, they are weightless
and we are just beginning.

1972

Un duque de Alba

Por más de veinte años
un duque de Alba
permaneció echado en su cama.
Entre la mugre de sus detritus
y la lepra de un amor desdichado,
veía salir el sol y ponerse,
veía, como una tumba más, la noche.
El aire mefítico que respiraba
mezclado venía con la fragancia
de los azahares de su amada.

A este duque de Alba, tan feliz,
lo envidiamos noblemente,
nosotros, en edad asolada
por la tecnocracia y la desconfianza.
Este duque de Alba tenía un solo
pensamiento, una idea, pero suya.
Lo iba gastando,
y al mismo tiempo enriquecía.
Pero nosotros, en varias camas,
con mugres y millones de lepras,
entre tecnologías dictatoriales,
planes y simulaciones,
ya no sufrimos nada.
Nos permiten tomar pastillas,
y callar.

1972

A Duke of Alba

For over twenty years
a duke of Alba
lay on his bed.
Amid the filth of his detritus
and the leprosy of wretched love,
he saw the sun rise and set,
he saw the night as one more grave.
The fetid air he breathed
blended with the fragrance
of his beloved's orange blossoms.

Happy as he was, we envy
nobly this duke of Alba,
we, who live in an age enlightened
by technocracy and mistrust.
This duke of Alba had one
thought, one idea, but it was his.
The more he spent it,
the richer he grew.
But we, in various beds,
with filth and millions of leprosies,
amid tyrannical technologies,
plans and simulations,
no longer suffer anything.
We are allowed to take pills,
and be silent.

1972

Alocución contra los necrófilos

De una vez y por todas: ¡a la mierda la muerte!
Mientras más me acerco a ella o ella a mí,
ni yo sé quién soy ni qué soy, le digo,
pero tú tampoco sabes quién ni qué eres.
El hombre te inventó o te dio nombre al menos,
tan sólo eso, que apenas si es algo,
una manera como tantas de infundir terror.
Pero conmigo eso no va, mi hermana.
Y menos, hacerle el juego a tus ritos.
Con los miles de millones de muertos
que conocemos, nuestra visión de ti
tendría que ser más bien risueña
o tan mecánica como la que ponemos
por ejemplo en el papel higiénico.
Si alguien osara en una noche
poblada de relámpagos, ululante el viento,
y todo el decorado de muerte chopiniana,
si alguien osara, digo, en medio de los suspiros,
coger al muerto por sus cabellos
igual que a una peluca inservible,
y decir, con voz muy natural:
ya no es como nosotros, y aquí, señores,
no ha pasado nada, ¡y siga la fiesta!
De modo que en vista de la muerte,
de la muerte natural por supuesto,
mucha naturalidad, tanta
que hasta el muerto se vuelva natural,
tan natural que se entierre o se queme
sin derramar una lágrima.
Tenemos que reservarlas
para cuando nos duelan las muelas.
Y si digo la muerte natural
es porque las provocadas

Against the Necrophiliacs

Once and for all, fuck death!
The closer I get to her or her to me
the less I know who or what I am. I tell her,
but you don't know who you are either.
Man invented you and gave you a name,
nothing more than that, which is hardly anything,
a way among many of spreading terror.
But that no longer works on me, sister.
And I don't take your rites seriously.
Given the thousands of millions of dead
we know, our vision of you
should be glorious
or as mechanical as our vision
of toilet paper, for example.
If someone dared on a night
full of lightning and howling wind,
the set decorated with Chopinesque death,
if someone dared, I say, in the midst of sighs
to take the dead man by the hair
as if he were wearing a useless wig,
and say very naturally:
he is no longer like us, ladies and gents,
don't worry yourselves about it, let the party continue!
So that given death,
natural death, of course,
let there be a lot of naturalness, so much
that even the dead man becomes natural,
so natural that we can bury him or burn him
without shedding a single tear.
We have to save our tears
for when we have a toothache.
And if I say natural death,
it's because the ones provoked

por la mano del hombre contra otro,
no han de ser lloradas por muerte
sino por vida que la vida
no segó a su hora.
No practiquemos el culto de los muertos,
¿acaso podemos pedirles
que practiquen el culto de los vivos?
La comunicación se ha cortado:
ni nos hablan ni nos oyen.
Hablemos pues con los vivos,
hasta que podamos.

1974

by the hand of one man against another
should not be mourned as death
but as life that life
did not sow at its proper time.
Let's not practice the cult of the dead.
Should we ask them
to practice the cult of the living?
Communication has been cut:
they don't speak to us or hear us.
Let's then speak to the living,
while we can.

1974

En resumen

Debo estar soñando
cuando alguien me dice:
«Escucha el veredicto».
Lleva careta de león,
y sus brazos con alas de águila.
De mármol negro son sus pies.
Le arranco la careta,
pero tras ella veo las fauces de la fiera.
Lo despojo de sus alas,
pero le nacen al instante otras más largas.
Le cerceno los pies,
pero son sustituidos por dos ventosas
que se pegan al piso.

Sucede que estoy naciendo,
y no es un sueño como presumía.
Durante nueve meses
soñé en el vientre de mi madre,
y ahora estoy en la realidad.
Al romperse la fuente placentaria
oigo de nuevo la voz decirme:
«Escucha el veredicto».

Por cierto,
Shakespeare, que engendró a Macbeth,
y lo parió con todo el dolor posible
–se desconocía en su época el parto sin dolor–,
se trasmutó en bruja de sí mismo
y le pronosticó al ambicioso:
«Tú serás rey»,
lanzó una carcajada shakesperiana
y volvió a ser Shakespeare.

In Brief

I must be dreaming
when someone tells me:
"Listen to the verdict."
He's wearing a lion mask
and his arms are eagle wings,
his feet are black marble.
I tear away the mask,
but behind it I see the maw of the beast.
I pull off its wings,
but instantly others, much larger, grow back.
I cut off its feet,
and in their place two suckers grow
that stick to the ground.

It happens that I'm being born,
and it's not a dream as I thought.
For nine months
I dreamed inside my mother's womb
and now I'm in reality.
When the water breaks
I hear that voice tell me once again:
"Listen to the verdict."

By the way,
Shakespeare, who engendered Macbeth,
and gave birth to him with the greatest pain—
in those days painless labor was unknown—
turned into a witch version of himself
and told the ambitious man:
"You will be king."
He gave a Shakespearean laugh
and became himself once more.

A ese hijo de taumaturgo
lo he visto en el teatro.
Nunca, y me hubiera gustado,
lo vi salir de la cabeza de su madre.

Así pues, habiendo salido de esa caverna
a las cinco de la madrugada
–hora lechosa, indecisa,
en que las brujas imaginarias
se confunden con las brujas reales–,
empecé a ser Virgilio.

Los egipcios tenían el *Libro de los Muertos*
para emprender el regreso al no ser,
pero nosotros, naciendo,
no disponemos de un *Libro de los Vivos.*
Toda madre
más que dar a luz, da a tinieblas,
y su fruto–topo desvalido–
engulle su primera ración de ceguera.

1975

I've seen that son of a magician
in the theater.
Much as I would have liked, I never
saw him come out of his mother's head.

And so, having left that cave
at five in the morning–
milky, uncertain hour
when imaginary witches
are confused with real ones–
I started becoming Virgilio.

The Egyptians had *The Book of the Dead*
to set out on their return to nonbeing.
but we, being born,
have no *Book of the Living*.
Every mother
gives more shadow than birth,
and her fruit–helpless mole–
swallows his first ration of blindness.

1975

Descansa, descansa

A César Bermúdez

Dilacerado, desunido, roto,
no puedes más, y yo siempre puedo.
Si das al tiempo una oportunidad, una sola,
sembrará ortigas en tu sangre.
Ahora, en la vasta extensión de esa pradera,
van cayendo uno a uno los recuerdos inmortales.
Una leona ayuntándose con un río
de estrellas negras. Por él navegan
los seres que nada esperan
en este mundo ni en el otro.

Nadie recuerda ya la forma
en que el sol se asomaba,
sólo la negrura en la cara.
Vamos donde nada existe,
vamos, tierra dorada,
de copas fúnebres
y cascos de caballos sin relincho,
vamos, a una velocidad fantástica,
hacia los arrozales de ese hombre
cuya gorra amarilla es como una declaración de amor.

¡Ay! Pero un ay que haga explotar
las cuatro paredes de ti mismo,
un ay capaz de engendrar
la sonrisa en tus labios marchitos
y puedas encaminarte hacia el templo de champán,
forrado de martas zibelinas y duendes verdes.

¿Cómo…? ¿Pero cómo? Si lo supieras…
Como se puede en la vida para poder en la nada.

Rest, Rest

for César Bermúdez

Lacerated, disjointed, broken,
you can't stand it any more, while I always can.
If you give time a chance, only one,
it will sow nettles in your blood.
Now, on the vastness of that prairie,
eternal memories fall.
A lioness mating with a river
of black stars. On it float
beings who expect nothing
of this world or the next.

No one remembers
how the sun peeked on the horizon,
only the blackness of its face.
Let's go where nothing exists,
let's go, golden earth
of funerary cups
and hooves of silent horses,
let's go at fantastic speed
toward the rice paddies of that man
whose yellow cap is like a declaration of love.

Ay! But let it be an *ay* that blasts away
the four walls of the self,
an *ay* capable of bringing
a smile to your withered lips,
that puts you on the path to the palace of champagne,
lined with marten fur and green *duendes.*

How?. . .But how? If you only knew
how one is able in life in order to be able in nothing.

Más tarde, entre tendales de gasa y abruptas confesiones,
el cómo de tu vida reirá a carcajadas.

No, no te dejo, no te suelto, no te desato.
Como un perro tendrás que...¿Aceptar?
Entre melocotones podridos y un guante caído de la mano
de la vieja dama, el cómo te dará un lanzazo.
Labial, palatalfricativa, gutural sonora,
sueña con tu lengua, sueña que es un misterio,
y morarás en esas alturas de focas desoladas.
La nieve empieza o va a empezar a caer, a caer
como el cadáver morado de un vigésimo piso.
Dale a tu lengua, hazla bífida, de serpiente,
acérala, tiémplala en la ortodoncia de tus dientes.
Menos y más, en la lengua, es el crucificado que esperamos.
Cuenta y narra, relata y expón los sortilegios
de la evidencia de una lengua en la palma de la mano.
Impetuoso relata hasta desintegrarte
en la dorada bruma de los días de tu dispersión.

La noche entra, dama enlutada y prostituta,
de coitos tan negros como sus telas.
Sus orgasmos traspasan la piel de los rinocerontes.
Allá, donde yo pongo el dedo, ¿no lo ves?
Allá es quien tiende la vista,
ese amigo lejano que te roe el corazón
cuando en las mañanas te lavas la boca.
En el allá que conoces nada hay que sembrar.
Unos cuantos insultos y unas medias rotas.

¿Cuándo? ¿Cuándo? En el mismo instante
en que lo piensas, todos los cuando
se alejan, vagones de un ferrocarril infinito,
trepidando, desolados, mordiendo el polvo.
Y tú en la estación del olvido, parado como una garza real,
gritas cuándo, cuándo, y la voz se te hace excremento.

Later, under gauze awnings and sudden confessions,
the how of your life will laugh raucously.

No, I won't leave you, I won't let you go, I won't untie you.
Like a dog you'll have to…Accept?
Among rotten peaches and a glove fallen from the hand
of an old lady, the how will strike you with its lance.
Labial, palatal fricative, voiced guttural,
dream of your tongue, dream it is a mystery,
and you will wander in those heights among desolate seals.
Snow begins or will begin to fall,
like a purple cadaver from a twentieth floor.
Hit your tongue, make it forked like a snake's,
stiffen it, temper it in the orthodontia of your teeth.
Less and more, on the tongue, is the crucified one we await.
Tell and narrate, relate and expose the magic spells
that give evidence of a tongue on the palm of your hand.
Tell the impassioned story until you fall apart
in the golden mist of the days of your dispersion.

Night enters, a prostituted lady in mourning,
with sex as black as her cloth.
Her orgasms pass through the skin of a rhinoceros.
There, where I point my finger, don't you see him?
There is the one who fixes his sight,
the distant friend who gnaws at your heart
when you brush your teeth in the morning.
In the far place you know there is nothing to sow.
A few insults, a few torn socks.

When? When? At the same instant
that you think it, all the when's
move away, cars of an infinite train,
shaking, desolate, chewing the dust.
And you on the station of oblivion, standing like a blue heron,
scream When? When? and your voice turns to excrement.

De qué entraña maldita a la recíproca unidad del latido
vas explorando ese camino incrustado entre muertos
al alcance de la mano.
Pero la loba de la casa amarilla
te entrega sus colmillos para que la devores:
ahora comienza el aquelarre de lo insustancial.
Río de agua sin agua, de palabras sin palabras,
inextinguible sed que aspira a convertirse en agua helada
y derramarse entre los vericuetos de tus vísceras.

Insustancialmente docto en un saber purulento,
letras semejantes a albaricoques hendidos por la espada,
irás a ocupar el infierno de los mudos.
¿Ángel caído? No, estercolero entrado en la gracia,
mística sangre pasada por diez millones de hectolitros
de asombro, verdeando en los girasoles del no ser.

La muy ilustre tonta se mece en una cuna de odio.
Se lamenta del hígado que le cuelga entre los senos.
Cuando en ese tren ilusorio
se sumerja entre las ruedas veloces,
determinará para todos el peso exacto del amor.

Allá y el cuándo entretanto se alejan
y atruenan el espacio con voces de piojos.
Han hurgado en las cabezas
y se echan a dormir en una cuna de tripas,
emocionados por haber entrevisto un reflejo de la vida.
Blandamente, acolchados,
algodón en rama, vientre deshilachado,
mineral fundido y goce obtuso, van a recoger a lo sumo
un grano de olvido en la suela de tus zapatos.
Todo se esfuma, obnubila y expande
en un gigantesco crustáceo tirado en esa playa de esqueletos.
Déjalo, no lo toques.
Sigue tu camino hacia la concha que resbala

From what damned entrails to the reciprocal unity of heart beats
do you go exploring that road lined
with the dead within your reach?
But the she-wolf of the yellow house
gives you her fangs so you can devour her:
now begins the coven of the insubstantial.
River of water without water, of words without words,
unquenchable thirst that hopes to become freezing water
and spill into the ins and outs of your guts.

Barely capable of purulent knowledge,
letters similar to apricots thrust open with a sword,
you will occupy the inferno of the mute.
Fallen angel? No, dung heap coming to grace,
mystical blood passed through ten million hectoliters
of surprise, turning green in the sunflowers of nonbeing.

The very illustrious fool rocks herself in a cradle of hate.
She complains about the liver that hangs between her breasts.
When she travels in that illusory train
and dives between speeding wheels,
she will define for all the exact weight of love.

Meanwhile the there and the when move away
and stun the air with the voices of fleas.
They've picked clean their heads
and fall asleep in a cradle of guts,
moved by having caught a glimpse of life's reflection.
Bland, comfortable,
cotton on the branches, disemboweled,
molten mineral and obtuse delight, they are to gather
at most a grain of oblivion in the sole of your shoes.
Everything goes up in smoke, grows dim and expands
into a gigantic crustacean lying on that beach of skeletons.
Let it be, don't touch it.
Follow the road to the conch that glides

en una espléndida mañana y decapítala.

La sangre de su cuello brota como una liberación anticipada.
Pasa un trineo conducido por un caballero astuto.
Suban, suban –dice, y todos suben.
Cómo, cuándo, allá pasan.
La madrépora se va mudando en mariposa,
y todos caen abruptamente en la nada.
Hasta mañana, amor mío.

1975

on the splendid morning and cut off its head.

Blood from its neck flows like a longed-for liberation.
A sleigh driven by an astute gentleman passes by.
Get on, get on, he says, and everyone gets on.
How, When, There go by.
White coral becomes a butterfly,
and everyone falls suddenly into the void.
Good night, my darling.

1975

Felizmente un camino

Escucha esas notas musicales
entre las cuerdas de un piano o de un arpa…
Notas, una por una,
cayendo en el debido sitio:
heridas inmortales que una vez abiertas
se convierten en flores, en flores o…
Pero no, no lo digas:
puede ocurrir que digas lo innombrable
y veas entonces el final del camino.
Del camino que nunca termina,
y camina sobre nosotros y con nosotros,
a veces tan ardientemente que el corazón se paraliza,
pero sólo un instante.
De pronto en Reina y Galiano
vas a Picadilly Circus en Londres,
o al doblar de la esquina en San Lázaro y Manrique
abruptamente estás en Piazza di Spagna.
Nada más natural: es el mismo camino:
no hay posible pérdida.

Cantando o llorando, caminas,
hermano mío de ruta, sin saber dónde.
Vamos, y otros vienen,
y nosotros venimos y otros van.
Las notas musicales nos acompañan
–lentas o veloces–, nos acompañan.
Quizá sepan dónde lleva el camino
y no lo preguntamos para no morir.

1975

Happily a Road

Listen to those musical notes
between the strings of a piano or a harp…
Notes falling, one by one,
in their proper place:
eternal wounds that open,
become flowers, flowers or…
But no, don't say it:
it might happen that you say the unsayable
and then see the end of the road,
the road that never ends,
and wanders over and with us
at times so ardently that the heart becomes paralyzed
but only for an instant.
Suddenly at the corner of Reina and Galiano
you find yourself in Piccadilly Circus,
or turning the corner of San Lázaro and Manrique
you're abruptly in the Piazza di Spagna.
Nothing more natural, it is the same road:
there's no way to get lost.

Singing or weeping you walk,
my fellow traveler, not knowing where.
We go, and some others come,
and we come and others go.
The musical notes go with us,
–slow or fast–they go with us.
Perhaps they know where the road goes
and we don't ask so we don't die.

1975

Himno a la vida mía

Loco de contento
me echo por esas calles,
huelo el perfume de la noche,
y grito: ¡Estoy vivo!
¿Acaso no se percatan?
Abro mi camisa, llevo la mano al corazón:
Oigan cómo late... No importa hasta cuándo.
Ahora vivo en medio de la calle,
y estoy de fiesta.
Mientras viva seré inmortal.
Si toco mi corazón,
es como si lo tocara eternamente.
Tan vivo estoy, que la historia
desfila ante mi vista,
y puedo acompañarla en su incesante marcha,
haber sido, ser y llegar a ser.
La sangre bulle en mis venas.
Cumple una y otra vez su ciclo,
y a la vida me aproxima más el tiempo.
Mía solamente, eterna en su bóveda celeste.
A este brazo que alzo, a esta boca que sonríe,
poder humano ni divino podrán darles
cristiana o pagana sepultura.
Desafían el negro boquete del sepulcro.
Aves de una especie desconocida,
sobre el polvo se encaminan intrépidos
hacia los mágicos espejos
donde la infinitud del tiempo
al hacerlos temporales, los reflejará en su pura esencia:
un brazo y una boca en mitad del planeta.
Obtener esta victoria
es la confirmación de estar vivo,
vivo siempre, abandonado

Hymn to My Life

Mad with happiness
I rush down the street,
I smell the perfume of evening
and I scream: I am alive!
Don't they notice?
I open my shirt, I place my hand on my heart:
Listen how it beats…It doesn't matter how long.
Now I live in the middle of the street,
and I'm having a ball
While I live I am immortal.
If I touch my heart,
it's as if I touched it forever.
I am so alive that history
parades before my eyes,
and I can go along on its incessant march,
to have been, to be, and get to be.
Blood boils in my veins.
It completes its cycle over and over
and time brings me closer to life.
Mine alone, eternal in its heavenly vault.
No human or divine power
will be able to give Christian or pagan burial
to this arm I raise, this mouth that smiles.
They defy the grave's black hole.
Birds of an unknown species
walk intrepidly on the dust
toward the magic mirrors
where infinite time, making them her own,
will reflect them in their pure essence:
an arm and a mouth in the middle of the planet.
To claim this victory
is proof of being alive,
always alive,

mi cadáver futuro,
para hablar con mi cuerpo y decirle: ¡Aleluya!

1976

my future corpse abandoned,
to speak to my body and say, Halleluiah!

1976

El hechizado

A Lezama, en su muerte

Por un plazo que no puedo señalar
me llevas la ventaja de tu muerte:
lo mismo que en la vida, fue tu suerte
llegar primero. Yo, en segundo lugar.

Estaba escrito. ¿Dónde? En esa mar
encrespada y terrible que es la vida.
A ti primero te cerró la herida:
mortal combate del ser y del estar.

Es tu inmortalidad haber matado
a ese que te hacía respirar
para que el otro respire eternamente.

Lo hiciste con el arma *Paradiso.*
–Golpe maestro, jaque mate al hado–.
Ahora respira en paz. Vive tu hechizo.

9 de agosto de 1976

The Magic Man

for Lezama, on his death

You have the advantage of death
over me by a handicap I cannot determine:
the same as it was in life, it was your fate
to come in first, I in second place.

It was written. Where? On the terrible
broiling sea that is life.
The wound closed over you first:
a battle to the death between being and not.

Your immortality rests in having killed
the one who kept you breathing
so that the other one could breathe forever.

You did it with the weapon *Paradiso*
--master stroke, destiny checkmated--.
Now breathe in peace. Your magic lives.

9 August 1976

Me esperan

Si es que hay tiempo
será para llegarme sólo
allí donde me esperan.
Y si me esperan,
no podría aceptar tu amor
ni el odio del otro
ni aún el sonajero
que un niño agita en mi oído.

They Are Waiting

If I have time
I'll use it to arrive alone
there where they await me.
And if they are waiting,
I can't accept your love
or another's hatred
or even the rattle
a child is shaking in my ear.

Y otro día

Y otro día va a comenzar,
otro día lleno de estopa,
de cartón y malestares.
En el pecho se vuelve plomo,
en la boca se me hace llanto,
en la cabeza oscuridades.
Estaba tan confundido
que la ciudad se hizo fango,
gigantes se hicieron los niños,
y los gigantes infrahumanos.
Salía por una puerta
y se presentaba otra puerta:
de tal modo que pregunté
lo que no puede contestarse.

Another Day

Another day will begin,
another day filled with fibrous waste,
cardboard and malaise.
In my chest the day turns to lead,
to weeping in my mouth,
darkness in my head.
I was so confused
that the city turned to mud,
children became giants
and the giants subhuman.
I went out one door
and came upon another:
and so I asked
what cannot be answered.

Naturalmente en 1930

Como un pájaro ciego
que vuela en la luminosidad de la imagen
mecido por la noche del poeta,
una cualquiera entre tantas insondables
vi a Casal
arañar un cuerpo liso, bruñido.
Arañándolo con tal vehemencia
que sus uñas se rompían,
y a mi pregunta ansiosa respondió
que adentro estaba el poema.

Naturally in 1930

Like a blind bird
flying in the light of the image
rocked by the night of the poet,
one of many bottomless ones,
I saw Casal
scratch a smooth, burnished body
with such force his nails broke,
and to my nervous question he responded
that inside that body was the poem.

De nuevo nacer

Ahí lo tienes sentado en su sillón,
tembloroso, indefenso, la mano que vacila
al coger el cigarro, con la mirada
en la que el tiempo depositó sus arenas.
Ahí lo tienes llamando con su voz aniñada
a los que ya se fueron para siempre.
Salmodia en un lenguaje incomprensible,
en tanto afuera se oyen voces graves.
¿Pero acaso las oye? ¿Dónde está ahora?
De regreso en el tiempo hasta la infancia
para balbucear, y al final orinarse.
Como en este momento en que lo ves
en un sillón, definitivamente solo.

1977

To Be Born Again

There you have him on his rocking chair,
trembling, defenseless. His hand shakes
as he reaches for a cigarette. In his eyes
time has deposited its sands.
There you have him calling with a childlike voice
those who have left forever.
He drones on in an unknown language,
while outside you can hear the grave voices.
Can he hear them? Where is he now?
He moves back in time to his infancy,
babbles and, in the end, pisses on himself,
as in this moment when you see him
on his rocking chair, totally alone.

1977

Dos o tres secretos

Para Fifi

Sólo muerto te confiaría
los dos o tres secretos
que todo hombre lleva en su pecho.
Mucho reirías
con tu risa metida entre los labios,
y yo reiría de mí sin miedo.
Muchacho, qué bobo has sido:
vivir tantos años
con dos o tres secretos.
Si te hubieras atrevido
no te quitaban el sueño y la alegría.
No los lleves a la tumba:
tanto respetar a los demás
o a ti mismo, no vale la pena.
Ahora que estás muerto
y también tus secretos,
si estuviera en mi poder
resucitarte, Virgilio,
cuáles son tus secretos, te preguntaría.
Y convertidos en polvo de chiste
podrías morir tranquilo.

1978

Two or Three Secrets

for Fifi

Only when I'm dead would I tell you
the two or three secrets
every man carries inside himself.
You'd laugh a lot
with your laughter stuck between your lips,
and I'd laugh at myself unafraid.
Boy, what a fool you've been:
to live that many years
hiding two or three secrets.
If you had dared,
those secrets wouldn't have robbed you
of all that sleep and joy.
Don't take them with you to the grave:
that much respect for others
or yourself is not worth it.
Now you're dead
along with your secrets.
If it were in my power
to bring you back, Virgilio,
I'd ask you what your secrets are.
Then they would become the brunt of jokes
and you could die in peace.

1978

Palabras de joven

Para Roberto Pérez,
en sus veintitrés años

Eternamente joven en su instante,
el joven pasea entre los lirios del camposanto,
y deja oír su tonada.
¡Oh, muertos! Estoy tan lleno de vida,
late en mi corazón, en mi frente.
Esplendo como un sol,
y tengo en la garganta un ruiseñor.

Se dispone a vivir, ¡oh, delicia!
El agua,
que no lava llagas en su piel,
la deja bruñida
como el escudo de Perseo.

Soy el mágico espejo
en que depositan sus sueños los amantes.
Cantadme himnos, alabanzas.
Soy un ensimismamiento para los sentidos,
y una fragancia para el alma.

El joven pasa desafiante.
Sol, luna, estrellas.
Yo soy la seducción. Vengan a adorarme.

1978

To a Young Man

For Roberto Pérez,
at twenty-three

Eternally young in an instant,
the young man strolls among the lilies of the graveyard.
Let's hear his song.
Oh, dead folk! I am so full of life,
it beats in my heart and my forehead.
I shine like a sun,
and there's a nightingale in my throat.

He gets ready to live, oh delight!
Water,
which doesn't wash the sores on his skin,
leaves it shining
like the shield of Perseus.

I am the magic mirror
in which lovers leave behind their dreams.
Sing me hymns and praises.
I am the senses' obsession
and a fragrance for the soul.

The young man passes, defiant.
Sun, moon, stars.
I am seduction. Come and adore me.

1978

Isla

Aunque estoy a punto de renacer,
no lo proclamaré a los cuatro vientos
ni me sentiré un elegido:
sólo me tocó en suerte,
y lo acepto porque no está en mi mano
negarme, y sería por otra parte una descortesía
que un hombre distinguido jamás haría.
Se me ha anunciado que mañana,
a las siete y seis minutos de la tarde,
me convertiré en una isla,
isla como suelen ser las islas.
Mis piernas se irán haciendo tierra y mar,
y poco a poco, igual que un andante chopiniano,
empezarán a salirme árboles en los brazos,
rosas en los ojos y arena en el pecho.
En la boca las palabras morirán
para que el viento a su deseo pueda ulular.
Después, tendido como suelen hacer las islas,
miraré fijamente al horizonte,
veré salir el sol, la luna
y lejos ya de la inquietud,
diré muy bajito:
¿así que era verdad?

1979

Island

Although I'm about to be reborn,
I won't proclaim it to the four winds
or feel like I am one of the chosen:
it happened by mere chance,
and I accept it because it's not in me
to deny myself, and, besides, it would be a discourtesy
a man of distinction would never commit.
I've been told that tomorrow
at six minutes after seven in the afternoon,
I will turn into an island,
as much an island as islands tend to be.
My legs will become earth and sea,
and gradually, just like a Chopin andante,
trees will grow out of my arms,
roses in my eyes, and sand in my chest.
In my mouth the words will die
so that the wind can blow at will.
Afterwards, lying down as islands tend to do,
I will stare at the horizon,
I will see the sun and moon rise,
and far then from the noise,
I will say very softly:
so it was true?

1979

de Poemas desaparecidos

from Disappeared Poems

Balada de tu muerte

Qué júbilo en tu cara
al llegar la quietud del soplo grave.
La casa, las vidrieras, las pinturas…
No hacían falta los ojos.
Las luces eran tintas negras
que no alumbraban nada.
Cantaba la alegría su canto ancho.
En escalas de risa
el viento nos besaba el alma.

Lo que es y será siempre;
final que torna a ser principio
de un final que se nutre de muerte,
vino hecho de luz
a plegar dulcemente su armonía,
ofrecimiento inmenso de mensajes lejanos.

Qué alborozo de voces
en tu muerte jocunda y diáfana,
sin convulsión de lágrimas
ni gentes aspirando tu aliento.

Ahora corremos en la ola que canta,
en un vuelo de alas, espiga en flor,
candor de niño y suavidad de nardos.
La única oración lanzada a la noche
en misterio, es ésta del retorno
al barro y a la arcilla, en forma humana.

1937

Ballad of Your Death

What joy in your face
when the quiet of the last breath arrived.
The house, the windows, the paintings…
Eyes were unnecessary.
The light was a black ink
shining on nothing.
Happiness sang its wide song.
The wind kissed our soul
in scales of laughter.

What is and will be always;
the end that becomes the beginning
of an end that is nourished by death
came made of light
sweetly folding its harmony,
a huge offering of distant messages.

What delightful voices
at your playful, diaphanous death,
without the heavy weeping
or people sucking up your breath.

Now we run on a singing wave,
in a flight of wings, a sprig of flowers,
candor of childhood and softness of a rose.
The only prayer hurled into the mystery
of night is that of return
to mud and clay, in human form.

1937

Los cencerros de la paciencia

Qué silenciosa la carretera
cuando sin eco
la van cruzando
los dos cencerros de la paciencia.

Qué triste el agua
cuando la sombra
pinta dos lomos sobre su tela.

Con su silencio la carretera
borda la angustia,
la angustia mansa
de los cencerros de la paciencia.

Un punto al aire
canta de pena,
y los dos belfos
arando soles,
el gesto inician de la paciencia.

Se abren caminos
de adormideras,
lunas de sueño,
rutas de estrellas.
Cinta de viento
sus lomos atan
y van volando
como luceros
los dos cencerros de la paciencia.

Camagüey, 1937

The Cow Bells of Patience

Such silence on the highway
when the two cow bells of patience
cross it without an echo.

Such sorrow on the water
when shadow paints the back
of two oxen on its cloth.

Silently the highway
embroiders the edge of anguish,
the tame anguish
of the two cow bells of patience.

A stitch in the air
sings of sorrow,
and the two snouts
plowing suns
begin the gestures of patience.

Paths open
through the poppies,
moon of dreams,
route of stars.
Ribbons of wind
tie the backs of the oxen
and, like morning stars,
the cow bells of patience go flying.

Camagüey, 1937

Ondean las largas banderas

Ha nacido el caballo salvador de los hombres.
Las largas banderas hinchadas de brisa.
La crin eriza y las vírgenes saludan.
¿Quién puede desconfiar en esta hora solemne?
El pez hirviente rechina en los estanques de incrédulos.
El caballo caracolea, se sienta en la mesa y las vírgenes lo cubren con sus túnicas.
Comed de mi carne, y el corazón muestra por entre la túnicas.
Bebed de mi sangre, y todo el mundo se vuelve a la inflamada púrpura de su lengua.
Ondean las largas banderas...
El caballo ha suprimido la vida entera.

Entre frutas pisoteadas y bandejas de plata, piafa y pita.
Piafa y pita entre los tabernáculos gigantes y cabezas de obispos.
Sus cuatro cascos sacan chispas de la cópula enana
que por la noche lame el papa para virilizarse.
Flamean los gallardetes por la sala del trono
colmada de monos calzados con elegantes zapatos y guantes blancos.
El ancla del arca brota de su boca llena de risa
de una risa que es un cauterio para las vírgenes.
Entre las aves muertas y los grandes asados,
los barcos con ojos de mujer y piel de tigre,
bajo el mantel repleto de cristalería que se pone en la cabeza
la enorme negra asomada a la ventana;
arriba, en las conchas que forma el fango que ahoga a la ciudad
siempre su lomo llevando a las vírgenes salva el mundo
y ordena las largas banderas.

Ha nacido el caballo salvador de los hombres.
Atrás el gori-gori, ánimas del purgatorio.
El caballo porta un espejo y todos se miran en el espejo;
el brillo de su aro mata a las ánimas
y el caballo emparrancado, se come una catedral.

Long Flags Waving

The horse–savior of men is born,
the long flags bloated with wind.
The mane bristles and the virgins salute.
Who can mistrust this solemn hour?
The boiling fish squeaks in the pond of the incredulous.
The horse half-turns, sits at the table and the virgins cover it with their tunics.
Eat of my flesh, and the heart appears inside the tunics.
Drink of my blood, and the whole world turns toward its swollen purple tongue.
Long flags waving…
The horse has abolished all of life.

Among flattened fruit and silver platters, the horse paws the ground and whistles.
It paws and whistles amid huge tabernacles and the heads of bishops.
Its four hooves throw off sparks from the tiny cupola
the pope licks at night to become manly.
The pennants flame in the throne room
packed with monkeys wearing elegant shoes and white gloves.
The ark's anchor spills from its mouth filled with laughter,
a laughter that singes the virgins.
Among the dead birds and the huge roasts
and ships with woman's eyes and skin of a tiger;
donning on her head the tablecloth covered with fine crystal,
the large black woman leans out the window;
above it all, on the mounds formed by the mud that drowns the city,
the horse carrying the virgins on its back saves the world
and brings order to the long flags.

The horse savior of men is born,
followed by the wail of souls in purgatory.
The horse carries a mirror in which everyone looks;
the gleam of its frame kills the spirits
and the bogged-down horse eats a cathedral.
Long flags bloated with wind…

Las largas banderas hinchadas de brisa...
Todo el mundo se convierte en un caballo,
en un caballo portado de la inmortalidad más deslumbrante,
en un caballo traspasador de vírgenes,
en un caballo perfectamente mortal.

Alguien se pone a gemir y el caballo lo devora al instante.
Enseguida se ve como dos caballos marchan por la calzada,
con grandes penachos y tiaras de arzobispos difuntos,
con coronas fúnebres cubiertas de hojaldre,
con lápidas funerarias empapadas en vino.
Ondean las largas banderas
por encima de las crines de los caballos humorísticos.

1944

Everyone turns into a horse,
a horse bearing the most blinding immortality,
a horse penetrator of virgins,
a perfectly deadly horse.

Someone begins to wail and the horse devours him instantly.
Immediately we see two horses marching down the avenue
with large crests and the miters of dead bishops,
with funeral crowns covered with dough
and headstones drenched in wine.
Long flags waving
over the manes of humorous horses.

1944

Nunca los dejaré

Cuando puso los ojos en el mundo,
dijo mi padre:
«Vamos a dar una vuelta por el pueblo».
El pueblo eran las casas,
los árboles, la ropa tendida,
hombres y mujeres cantando
y a ratos peleándose entre sí.
Cuántas veces miré las estrellas.
Cuántas veces, temiendo su atracción inhumana,
esperé flotar solitario en los espacios
mientras abajo Cuba perpetuaba su azul,
donde la muerte se detiene.
Entonces olía las rosas,
o en la retreta, la voz desafinada
del cantante me sumía en delicias celestiales.
Nunca los dejaré—decía en voz baja;
aunque me claven en la cruz,
nunca los dejaré.
Aunque me escupan,
me quedaré entre el pueblo.
Y gritaré con ese amor que puede
gritar su nombre hacia los cuatro vientos,
lo que el pueblo dice en cada instante:
«Me están matando pero estoy gozando».

1962

I'll Never Leave Them

When he turned his eyes to the world
my father said:
"Let's take a walk around town."
The town was the houses,
the trees, the clothes hanging from the line,
men and women singing,
at times fighting among themselves.
Many times I looked at the stars.
Many times, afraid of their unhuman attraction,
I hoped to float solitary in space
while below was the eternal blue of Cuba,
where death dared not enter.
Then I smelled the roses,
and from the open air concert the out-of-tune voice
of a singer drowned me in heavenly delights.
I'll never leave them—my father said softly,
even if they crucify me,
I'll never leave them.
Even if they spit on me,
I'll stay among my people.
And I'll shout with that love that can shout
its name to the four winds,
what the town says moment to moment:
"They're killing me but I'm having fun."

1962

En el dentista

¿Qué puede hacerse contigo? ¿Qué podría encontrar tu frescura en mi piel ajada?
Te engalanas para el amor, gimes por el amor, te hundes en su noche.
Quizás no sepas quiénes fueron Baudelaire y la señora Sabatier, ni lo que entre ellos ocurrió. Pero es tan divertido (o tal vez sea otra cosa) escribir estos renglones dedicados a ti, que para mí no eres más que un fantasma.

1965

At the Dentist

What to do with you? What could your freshness find
in my worn-out skin?
You primp yourself up for love, you moan for love, you drown
in its night.
Perhaps you don't know who Baudelaire and Mme. Sabatier were,
or what happened between them. But it's so much fun
(or perhaps it's something else) to write these lines dedicated to you,
who are for me nothing but a ghost.

1965

Pin, pan, pun

El niño me mató con su fusil de palo. Muerto empecé a verlo
en su lento crecimiento hacia la crueldad.
En estos días me gusta escuchar los disparos. Se tiñe
de sangre el horizonte. Todos afirmamos que la felicidad
es una bala.

1969

Shooting Gallery

The boy killed me with his wooden gun. Dead, I began to see him
growing slowly toward cruelty.
These days I like to listen to gun shots. The horizon
turns the color of blood. We can all affirm that happiness
is a bullet.

1969

Quien soy

Poco importa mi nombre, y mucho menos mi edad.
No he de enumerar la caída del pelo ni decir «encanezco».
Tan sólo una sencilla confesión: no tengo ni un perro acompañante,
y tengo cantidades de soledad que regalar.

1969

Who I Am

My name matters little and my age matters less.
I won't mention my hair falling out or say it is "graying."
Just a simple confession: I don't even have a dog as companion,
and I have plenty of solitude to give away.

1969

Una niñada de Piñera

Para Ana María Muñoz

Querida, no dijiste que hoy es tu natalicio, y que soñaste subir penosamente los escalones del templo del Dolor; tampoco aseveraste que se te quemó el pastel de pollo. Ni siquiera te pasa por la mente dónde irá a parar el humo de esa chimenea que sobresale por entre árboles esqueléticos; ni que esta tarde el aire te trae el recuerdo de otra vida; ni que yo, como un perro desvalido, ladro al fantasma de mi desesperación.
Ana María,
esta divagación me ayuda a soportarme; como un niño malcriado hundo el dedo en el helado de fresa, interrumpo la conversación de los mayores, enumero en voz alta las verrugas de mi madre…
Ana María,
ayúdame a salir de mí. Llévame por ese camino interminable a la quietud de un esplendor permanente.

1973

Piñera's Inner Child

for Ana María Muñoz

My dear, you didn't say today was your birthday and that you dreamed of going up
the difficult steps to the temple of Sorrow; nor did you admit
that you burned the chicken pie. You can't even imagine where the smoke
might go from that chimney rising among the skeletal trees; or that this afternoon
the breeze brings you the memory of another life; or that I, like a wretched dog
bark at the ghost of my despair.
Ana María,
these ramblings help to me to tolerate myself; like an ill-behaved
child, I stick my finger into the strawberry ice cream, I interrupt adults when
they talk, I count out loud
my mother's warts...
Ana María,
help me escape myself. Take me down that endless road
to the quietness of permanent splendor.

1973

¿Se dijo?

¿Se dijo o no se ha dicho?
Oíamos entretanto la música, acompañada del piafar de los caballos. Un modo de eludir las enojosas preguntas.
Con todo, si se ha dicho o no, me preocupa.
¿Te acuerdas del sentido?
Si carece de sentido, callaremos.
¿Callar, se puede?
De cada lengua salen pistas de aterrizaje, hacia las pistas practicadas en los oídos. Callar sería catastrófico: secaría la emoción. Las palabras no podrían despegar.
—Dime si ya se dijo. Quizá recuerdes una palabra. Lánzala de tu rampa de despegue. Lánzala hacia este oído, que se está muriendo por oír.
Tu silencio llena mi pecho con vacíos pintados de cal.
Blanco, esparcido blanco.
Si te obstinas en callar, sin una mancha estará mi alma.
Enviléceme: habla.
Dime cuatro verdades.
Necesito tu voz y tu verbo.
Deberé luego hundir un puñal en tu pecho.

1976

Was It Said?

Was it said or was it not?
In the meantime we heard music accompanied by the clopping
of horses. A way of eluding annoying questions.
On top of that, it worries me whether it's been said or not.
Do you remember the sense of it?
If it makes no sense, we'll be quiet.
To be quiet, is that possible?
Landing strips spread from each tongue
toward the usual strips in our ears. To be quiet would be catastrophic:
it would dry up emotion. Words couldn't take off.
Tell me if it's already said. Perhaps you might remember a word. Hurl it
from your launching pad. Hurl it toward this ear, which
is dying to hear.
Your silence fills my chest with a white-washed void.
White, well-spread white.
If you're determined to be quiet, my soul will be without a stain.
Degrade me: speak.
Tell me four truths.
I need your voice and your word.
Then I'll have to stick a dagger in your chest.

1976

De sobremesa

¿Qué cosa, tú?
Con su problema, su lástex y sus pulseras, se sienta a la mesa:
Aquí estoy.
Desde otra mesa:
Aquí estoy.
Desde el fondo:
Aquí estoy.
Semejante a un astro pavo, relleno de palabras, brilla con luz propia: aquí estoy.
María, Luis, Jaime, Rebeca, Jorge.
Frituras de seso, sopa de fideos, *gateaux á la crême.*
Eres un falso. Qué vida esta. Mañana será otro día.
A Rebeca le nació un niño deforme. Qué ricas las frituras. Debo ir al velorio de mi primo. No le pongas tanta sal a la ensalada.
Contra todo lo esperado nadie grita ni se apagan las luces.

¿Quién dijo miedo? El miedo con los ojos desorbitados y una albóndiga atravesada en la garganta. ¿Quién dijo miedo?
¿Quién en esta hora de tinieblas, olvida alisar la raya de su pantalón? ¿Quién, con sonrisa encantadora y la yema del dedo, no desprende el grano de arroz caído en la solapa de su saco?
El miedo, que viste y calza nuestros actos, se sienta a la mesa con nosotros.
Aquí estoy.
¿Saldrá expulsado, entre restos de albóndigas y frituras, por cada uno de los anos?
Música. Luces cegadoras. Empieza a acariciarme. Dime que soy tu niño. Arrópame. Cuéntame el cuento del pie que habla y de la cabeza que camina. Recuérdame el sol que vimos juntos.
Señálame el barco con tu dedo otra vez. Asegúrame que iremos esta noche a una función del ratón Mikito.
Suave, suave.
Derivando.

Table Talk

What is it, you?
She sits at the table with her problems, her Lastex and her bracelets:
Here I am.
From another table:
Here I am.
From the back:
Here I am.
Similar to an astral turkey, stuffed with words, the phrase
shines with its own light: here I am.
María, Luis, Jaime, Rebeca, Jorge.
Brain fritters, noodle soup, *gateaux à la crème.*
You're a liar. What a life. Tomorrow is another day.
Rebeca gave birth to a deformed child. These fritters are delicious. I must
go to my cousin's funeral. Don't put so much salt on the salad.
No one screams at what's expected, nor do the lights go out.

Who mentioned fear? Fear with eyes bulging
and a meatball in the throat. Who mentioned fear?
In this hour of darkness who forgets to iron his pants?
Who will not, with a charming smile, remove
the grain of rice stuck to his lapel with the tip of his finger?
Fear, disguised by our behavior, sits at the table
with us.
Here I am.
Will it be expelled from each of our anuses
along with bits of meat balls and fritters?
Music. Blinding lights. Come and caress me. Tell me I'm
your baby. Clothe me. Tell me the story of the foot that speaks
and the head that walks. Remind me of the sun we saw together.
Point to the ship again. Assure me that tonight we'll go
to a Mickey Mouse show.
Soft, soft.
Meandering.

¿Cuánto nos falta para llegar al antes? Deslízame.
Suave, suave.
¿A qué distancia estamos?

Ten cuidado. Vas a pisar la fritura que ha dejado caer el señor de la gardenia en la solapa. O del grano de arroz en la solapa. Suave, mi amor. Suave. No me cuentes más. Ya no hace falta. Ahora sácame el rabito, que me hago pipí.

1977

How much longer before we get to before? Slide me down.
Soft, soft.
How far are we?

Be careful. You're about to step on the fritter dropped by the man
with a gardenia on his lapel. Or with the grain of rice on his lapel.
Soft, my love. Soft. Don't say anything else. It's no longer necessary.
Now pull out my pipi. I have to go.

1977

Nadie

Cada vez que el empleado levanta la sábana que cubre tu
cuerpo, el que mira exclama: Nunca lo he visto.
Tuviste amigos, una esposa, hijos, jefes y subordinados.
Todos desfilan. Escrutan tu cara, y suponiendo que podrías ser
al que amaron u odiaron, se consternan ante tu calculada
inescrutabilidad.

1977

No One

Each time the attendant raises the sheet covering your body,
the observer exclaims: I've never seen him before.
You had friends, a wife, children, bosses and employees.
They all pass by. They study your face, and supposing you
might be the one they loved or hated, they are frustrated
by your inscrutable calculus.

1977

Notes on the Poems

"The Weight of the Island"

Areíto: A Taino religious feast.

Ñáñigo: A member of the Abakuá secret society in Cuba.

Tres: A traditional Cuban string instrument related to the guitar. It has three courses of two strings each.

Clave: Clave refers to the traditional beat underlying all of Cuban music. In the plural it refers to a pair of wooden sticks, usually made of mahogany, which sets the clave beat.

"The Garden"

Zenea: Juan Clemente Zenea (1832- 1871), Cuban poet and patriot. He is said to have introduced Romanticism to Cuba.

Casal: Julián del Casal, (1863 – 1893), Cuban poet, forerunner of Latin American Modernism.

Dos Ríos: Battle of Dos Ríos, 1895, during which José Martí, Cuba's greatest patriot and poet, was killed by Spanish forces.

"Happily a Road"

Reina and Galiano: a popular street corner in Havana.

San Lázaro and Manrique: a popular street corner in Havana.

Biographies

Virgilio Piñera was born in Cárdenas, Cuba, in 1912 and died in Havana in 1979. He lived in Argentina for twelve years and collaborated in *Sur*, the magazine that Jorge Luis Borges directed. He befriended many Argentine writers, among them Borges, Adolfo Bioy Casares, and the Polish writer Witold Gombrowicz, who was then in self-imposed exile in Argentina. Piñera published his first novel, *La carne de René*, in Buenos Aires. Besides poetry, he wrote many plays, among them *Electra Garrigó, En esa zona helada, Falsa alarma,* and *Dos viejos pánicos*. He also wrote short fiction, collected in *Cuentos fríos*, and, posthumously, in *Cuentos completos*. Currently, he is considered one of the great Cuban writers of the 1950s, alongside José Lezama Lima and others, who collaborated in the magazine *Orígenes*.

Pablo Medina was born in Havana, Cuba, in 1948. He is the author of fourteen books of poetry, fiction, non-fiction, and translation. Most recently, he collaborated with photographer Carlos Ordoñez on a collection of poetry and photography titled *Calle Habana* (PhotoStroud, 2013). His novel *Cubop City Blues* (Grove, 2012) appeared in paperback in 2013. Winner of various awards, among them grants from the Rockefeller, Oscar B. Cintas and Guggenheim foundations, the state arts councils of New Jersey and Pennsylvania, the NEA, the Lila-Wallace Reader's Digest Fund, and others, Medina is professor in the Department of Writing, Literature and Publishing and directs the MFA Program at Emerson College in Boston.

Made in the USA
Lexington, KY
02 July 2019